THE LOST LAKE

THE LOST LAKE

Evidence of prehistoric boat building

Stephen Clarke

With contributions by
Peter Bere, John and Jane Bray, Gordon McDonald,
Neil Phillips

Monmouth Archaeological Society
2013

The Lost Lake

Typeset, printed, bound and published by Clarke Printing, Monmouth

ISBN 978-0-9558242-2-7

For my grandson
who has brought great joy

ACKNOWLEDGEMENTS

Without the help and enthusiasm of Jane and John Bray, Peter Bere and Gordon McDonald this book would never have been.

Charles Boase has produced the Index, read and advised on the text – his help and advice has been indispensable.

Rhodri, my son, and Ellie, have done their best to introduce me to the digital age – I fear with little success.

I am grateful for the interest shown by Professor Bill Manning, Professor Alasdair Whittle, Professor Ray Howell Dr Adam Gwillt, Dr Elizabeth Walker, the Late Doctors Paul and Yolanda Courtney, Dr Neil Phillips, Nick Ramsay AM, Jeremy Knight, Dennis Lofhagen (photographer), Colin Harris and Felicity Taylor, David Harrison, Phil Riches Sue, Ted and Melanie Chivers, Paul Davies, Stuart Wilson, Ann Leaver, Martin Tuck, Reg Jackson, Reg Clarke, Philomena and Martin Goodall, Vic Powles, Dave Pritchard, Dave Hancocks, Lyn Harper, Neil Maylan of GGAT, Lindsay Ward; Andrew Helme, Sue Miles and friends at Monmouth Museum; our President Sox and the late Keith Kissack, Geoff Webb with our erudite friends at GCHQ Overmonnow and, of course, my understanding wife, Hazel. Special thanks must go to Professor Francesco Menotti for his encouragement from afar.

Finally, I am most grateful to the leaders and workmen on the Parc Glyndŵr site for their unstinting and good-natured support during two years of ice, snow, gales and blazing heat: MD Steve Williams, Site Manager Ashleigh Williams, Phil Champion, Brian and Kerry Hughes and team and David Jones.

All of Randalls' boys at Parc Glyndŵr were inspired by the archaeology and their leader, Antony, was a constant supporter in all things; so many thanks to him and his team of Lewis, Sky, Colin, Richard, Carl, Stuart, and Fletcher, without them the results of the project would have been far from complete.

A NOTE

When we unearthed the three linear features running across one of six Bronze Age burnt mounds at Parc Glyndŵr Gordon McDonald and Jane Bray immediately suggested that the remains could be associated with prehistoric boat building. However, to their frustration, it took almost a year for me to accept their interpretation . . . and the conversion came slowly. Admittedly, from the start, the 'channels' looked like twin canoes with an outrigger but I thought they were more likely to be structural foundations and rashly gave the Press a 'longhouse mystery'.

However, the evidence built-up that the channels formed a framework for boat building – boat-shaped twin canoe channels; outrigger shaped channel; the perfectly parallel and the perfectly level nature of the channels; their clear association and right-angled junction with the lake; their close association with the abandonment of the Bronze Age burnt mound; the strong evidence for woodworking in the channels; the evidence for the channels being a seasonal activity on the shore of the lake; the rock art evidence for Bronze Age boats with outriggers; the ethnographic evidence for canoes with outriggers; the evidence for the continuity of boat building techniques at Smallhythe in Kent and now the recognition of the features on the Bronze Age Lurgan boat in Ireland.

If our interpretation is correct, the remains at Parc Glyndŵr are of international significance. Of course such discoveries should first be published in an academic journal – after the Press have played with whatever 'First' or 'Biggest' or 'Best Preserved' the excavators have passed around. Later, one might produce a popular book, perhaps.

I have decided to do it the other way around – for several reasons – but primarily because large areas of the post-glacial lake and its shores adjoining Parc Glyndwr are under imminent threat from development. Secondly, I'm getting on a bit and might not survive long enough to see a paper pass through the tender hands of peer reviewers. Had I used Occam's Razor I may have accepted the obvious interpretation by Gordon McDonald and Peter Bere a year ago.

Although this study is based on normal archaeological techniques and scientific dating I have not attempted to produce an archaeological report in a form which will satisfy all of my colleagues. One of my old friends who abandoned the discipline long ago commented to me that he had so seldom heard one archaeologist 'say anything good about another's interpretation of so many things' – so I don't expect too much.

However, I hope that other archaeologists will look seriously at the evidence, for someone may well have seen similar features in similar situations elsewhere. Because sites all around Parc Glyndŵr are being developed I have written more for the layman – especially for the people of Monmouth – the ones who may well have to defend the archaeology.

CONTENTS

*Although Monmouth is 18 miles from the Severn Estuary
the medieval town Seal is of a ship*

ON THE SHORES OF A LOST LAKE

THIS book is about the discovery of the remains of a huge post-glacial lake and of the people living on its shores. The Monmouth lake was a larger body of fresh water than any in southern Wales today and with Stone Age to Iron Age activity along its banks it would be incredible if there had been no ancient lacustrine activity out on the lake itself.

Travelling on water is one of the oldest of human activities as is shown by prehistoric rock art and the many preserved dugouts and a dozen Bronze Age boat planks scattered around these islands. However, as far as we know, no-one in Western Europe has ever recognised a prehistoric 'boatyard'. Consequently, no-one could say precisely what one should have been looking for – especially as traditional ideas of medieval boat building have recently proved to have been so very wide of the mark.

But, if we look at technologies of the past, perhaps there are clues. Over most of human history needs have been similar (farming the land, transport, grinding corn, metalworking, pottery, spinning and weaving, weaponry and so on). Consequently, until the Industrial Revolution most technologies changed very little, sometimes over millennia.

The only early boat building sites we know of are the medieval ones at Poole in Dorset and Smallhythe in Kent where excavations failed to produce any of the expected features. If the continuity idea holds true we might reasonably assume that similar systems to those revealed on those sites could have been used during earlier times – perhaps even in prehistory.

The requirements on rivers, lakes and oceans were the same throughout history – craft which would carry people and goods – craft that had to be constructed on land and launched from land.

Neither at Smallhythe nor Poole were there any of the expected inlets to the estuary or enclosed docks as vessels were constructed in channels dug into the ground and shaped like the bottoms of the boats or ships being made. The channels were aligned along the bank of the estuary just above high tide level and at right angles to the water, with level bases upon which keels could be laid.

At Monmouth, two 30 metre long perfectly parallel channels, shaped like the bottoms of log boats, were discovered lying across a burnt mound; the mound produced a radiocarbon date and pottery of the Bronze Age. The channels were set just above the water level of the lake and although far smaller, they were in other ways identical to the boat-shaped channel at Smallhythe. The Monmouth channels were aligned along the edge of the lake at right angles to the water and had very level bases, as did the one at Smallhythe. The water level of the Monmouth lake suggests that the channels could have been purposely flooded from the lake or at least easily filled with water brought from the lake bank.

Well over a hectare of ground (10,000 square metres) in the immediate vicinity of the channels was excavated or landscaped with a grading bucket under archaeological control; this proved conclusively that the channels were isolated and not part of some agricultural or water management system. Far larger adjoining areas were also stripped during the removal of peat or trenched during the construction of 85 houses and once again no comparable features were revealed.

At Monmouth there was a third parallel, but differently shaped, channel – the whole having the appearance of being the base for some form of precisely constructed framework. The evidence for wood working at Smallhythe came from ships nails in the channels while at Monmouth – some three thousand years earlier – it came from sharp flakes of imported flint, mostly found along the sides of the channels. On both sites, especially if the channels were flooded, the completed vessels could have been slid straight out on to the lake or, of course, hauled up out of the water; however, the length and precisely parallel nature of the channels makes it unlikely that they were the result of beaching. The remains were sealed by thousands of years of silting turned to clay.

The chances of finding a preserved combination vessel of the kind suggested by the remains is far lower than finding the more unstable single-hulled craft – of which scores have been preserved around Western Europe. This is probably due to the survival value of any combinations which would more often end life against dry land and have been broken up for spares or for firewood. Also, it appears that at least part of one has been found – at Lurgan in Ireland – one of considerable interest when considering the Monmouth matrix. The Lurgan boat has a series of paired holes which the authors say can only be explained as fixing points for the attachment either of another logboat or stabilisers or an outrigger of some kind and they consider it likely to have been a sea-going vessel.

The Lurgan boat is a huge 15 metres long and 1.0 metre wide. Part of a second similar vessel was found nearby at Carrowneden. Both the Irish boats are of a similar period to the Monmouth burnt mound cut by the channels: The Lurgan boat radiocarbon date was 3940 ± 25 BP and the Carrowneden one 3890 ± 80 BP. The radiocarbon dates obtained from the Bronze Age Burnt Mound 3 which is the one cut by the Parc Glyndŵr channels is 3700 ± 35 BP and it is also interesting that Channel 3 is the same width as the Lurgan boat.

Twin hulled craft with outriggers, as those envisaged at Parc Glyndŵr, were still in use in Fiji during the 19th century.

However, the case for lacustrine or even maritime activity at Parc Glyndŵr does not rest solely on the linear remains on the lakeside. The supporting evidence for boat-building is extensive and there does not appear to be a more feasible or realistic interpretation. Away from Parc Glyndŵr other parts of the lake shore and its levels have been recorded and dated; the situation and height of the features overlooking the shallower water has been established; the proliferation of prehistoric sites along the waterside – with dating – has been ascertained; the lake was surrounded by heavy woodland for raw materials and there is ample plastic clay. And there are the three rivers feeding the lake. All this is supported by ethnographic and other evidence for combined canoes and outriggers and by the considered opinions of several maritime archaeologists.

During the 19th century sea-going boats were again built in Monmouth and launched into the River Wye – but this time they were up to 400 tons in weight. So it is evident that if Bronze Age boats had gained tidal access over the post-glacial blockage of the Wye Valley, or been beached and re-floated below it, they could easily have reached the sea.

INTRODUCTION

THE counties of Hereford, Gloucester and Gwent meet in the Wye Gorge between Monmouth and Ross-on-Wye where the river is overlooked by limestone cliffs, prehistoric caves, and the great Iron Age hillfort of the Little Doward. Here, as you cross the border into Wales, the valley suddenly opens to reveal a panoramic bowl edged by wooded hills, with Monmouth set on rising ground, where three rivers meet. The Wye, the Monnow and the Troddi are some of the most beautiful rivers in the world but as they pass serenely by the town one forgets the occasional dramatic floods and that Monmouth was once a Roman and medieval iron-working centre and where 19th century ocean-going boats were built and launched to faraway seas. Also, few people realise, while standing in Monnow Street to view our famous medieval bridge, that almost into historic times, one would have been standing in at least six metres of water – for the Monmouth basin had once been filled with one of the largest and deepest of prehistoric lakes.

ELSA SEARLE, formerly Geography Mistress at St Julians High School in Newport produced (in 1970) a masterly geomorphological study of the rivers of Monmouthshire, for which all local archaeologists should be grateful. The work includes a definitive study of the geology of the Monmouth basin and sets the background scene to a huge prehistoric lake and the archaeological discoveries and interpretations recorded in this book.

Monmouth town sits on a spur of the First and Second Gravel Terraces and is almost surrounded by a huge spread of gravel and alluvium stretching from the gorge above Redbrook for about two miles up the Wye, Monnow and Troddi Valleys. Part of the basin is floored with the soft Raglan Marls but also partly underlain by the St Maughan's Group which forms land over 300 feet high in other areas of the county. Elsa Searle points out that the Monmouth basin cannot, therefore, be attributed to differential erosion alone.

The first of the two gravel terraces rises to the south and north of the wide plain of alluvium while the second terrace is restricted to the northern parts of Monmouth – about 90 metres above the river. Searle suggests that this may be the equivalent in age of the Boyne Hill Terrace of the Thames Valley which was probably cut in the Great or Hoxnian Interglacial Period (250,000 years ago to 200,000 years ago).

This means that the terrace was formed after the Lowestoft Glaciation (350,000 years ago to 250,000 years ago). Terrace 1 is only 10 to 12 feet above the river and is much later in age – probably dating from the period after the York Glaciation (26,000BC to 13,000BC). Much of Monmouth is built on this terrace – which is well above all modern flood levels. A narrow band of Terrace 2 extends northwards to Rockfield through a dry gap rising to 122 feet.

Searle continues:

> This large basin appears to have been excavated by ice at some period, most probably during the maximum glaciation – the Lowestoft. Ice moving down the Monnow Valley and ice through the Mitchel Troy gap may have collected here and perhaps some from the Wye, although it is difficult to imagine that ice could cope with the extraordinary incised meanders of the river above Monmouth.
>
> The ice may have collected in such quantities that only a part of it could escape along the Wye below Monmouth and gradually a deep hollow would be gouged out. When the ice retreated, water would lie in the hollow and a lake form. The lake seems to have persisted for some time and then the level fell and lacustrine deposits at a lower level were laid down. The large amounts of alluvium may represent a third level in fairly recent times. A westerly spread of Terrace 2 to Baily Pit Farm where there is no river valley does suggest that the terraces are not of river origin. The dry valley leading to Rockfield is above the level of the higher terrace and was most probably excavated by an ice tongue at some period. The form of the meanders of the Monnow does not fit in with the possibility that it was once part of a meander.

If the Monmouth basin had been the site of a vast lake which had been formed at the end of the last Ice Age, we must ask what physical evidence remains today. The aspects of a post-glacial lake which need to be established are: if there are any traces of the late Ice Age blockage of the Wye Valley; the extent of the lake; its depth; the period of its draining; and, if possible some dates. Significantly there is archaeological evidence for all four.

The late Ice Age blockage of the Wye Valley: the primary reason for the post-glacial lake and its survival was the existence of the Wye Gorge below Monmouth. Here the valley closes significantly and at its narrowest point the debris from the melting glacier must have accumulated sufficiently to hold back the vast body of melt-water which built up in the Monmouth basin. The location of the obstruction seems to be recorded by the Colman Rocks in the bed of the Wye and by an associated moraine on the Welsh bank of the river (SO 53312 10382). There are no similar features to these – the rocks or the moraine – in this part of the Wye Valley.

The extent of the lake is, of course, related to its depth and it is suggested that alluvial deposits of sand, gravel and pebbles at some 21m OD around the upper parts of Monmouth which were associated with prehistoric human activity had marked the shoreline of the lake. If this is correct, then the body of water would have extended a long way out across the alluvium towards the Parc Glyndŵr development site. One of the unanswered questions was how much higher the water had to be above the 21m OD level, in order to deposit graded sand, gravel and pebbles which have been found and been pre-dated in Monnow Street and St James' Street.

The speculation was ended when the bed of the lake at Parc Glyndŵr was firmly established to be around 23m OD and the lake shown to have survived into the later Iron Age. There was no barrier known between Parc Glyndŵr and the gorge above Redbrook, so it is easy to establish what the minimum level of water would have been in the town – and it was rather stunning – for most of Overmonnow and lower Monmouth would have been under at least six metres of water. The lake would have extended at least up to Agincourt Square with at least two metres of water covering the two dated contexts in Monnow Street and St James' Street – presumably ample, especially during flooding, to have carried the material sealing the prehistoric contexts.

Geologists seemed unsure of just how long the lake had survived after the melting of the ice sheets; for instance, Searle, as noted, just says that it 'seems to have persisted for some time' (Searle, *ibid*) while Dreghorn says nothing on the issue (Dreghorn, 1968). On the other hand, McDonald suggests that it had not drained until the Bronze Age, or even later (McDonald, 2011).

The archaeological evidence obtained from the alluvial deposits along the suspected shores inside Monmouth town is more specific and suggests that the lake had survived into the late Iron Age – the 1st century BC. The shores of the lake – running around the 1st and 2nd Gravel Terraces – would have extended across the alluvium to the Parc Glyndŵr development site, thus creating a lake larger than any in southern Wales today.

Other dating evidence from the shoreline of the lake comes from a water-worn Early Bronze Age barbed and tanged flint arrowhead found sealed in the alluvial gravels in upper Monnow Street (No 24 – Site 1). There is also the substantial assemblage of worked flints from a Mesolithic camp site as well as late Iron Age pottery and a radiocarbon date from beneath graded alluvial deposits in St James' Street (outside No 4 – Site 2). At Parc Glyndŵr animal bones on the bed of the lake, which must pre-date the draining of the lake and the subsequent silting up of the residual lagoon, produced a radiocarbon date of c525 BC.

Subsequent deposits show that the lake had drained and the lagoon was being silted up during Roman times when a radiocarbon date from the peat in the lagoon was dated to cAD 195 and a sherd of Samian Ware from the anaerobic clay over the peat was dated by Peter Webster to cAD 140-200. Support for Iron Age or Roman activity on the site came (as going to Press) when a stream channel was discovered cutting the lagoon remains (west) deposits with bloomery iron slag in the primary sediment.

Also, although prehistoric material is widespread in plough soil around the Monmouth basin, it is mostly absent below about the 20m contour where Roman remains, especially of iron working, are very common. The exceptions are microliths found in the silts of the alluvium, especially during excavations in Monnow Street, which can presumably be explained as harpoon barbs lost by hunter-gatherers out on the lake.

At Parc Glyndŵr the bed of the lake by the early Iron Age had risen to over 23m OD – actually a little higher than the adjoining Bronze Age level of the land. However, the dropping of flood silts along the lakeside had caused the land around the lake to remain above the water level and, by the time of the draining of the lake, over a metre of flood silts had turned to firm clay over the lake and the Bronze Age levels. This apparently indicates that the level of the lake, except when it was in flood, was close to the 23m OD, a suggestion that would support the idea that the extensive human activities overlooking the lake were carried out during the summer months as the banks would have been very boggy or flooded during the winter. It also supports the suggestion that the activities were likely to have been closely associated with the lake.

The digging of a modern flood attenuation pond beside the shore of the ancient lake was to expose a series of prehistoric sites with some 700 years of Bronze Age occupation and a Stone Age hearth a thousand years earlier – all within an area 30 metres long. With the Iron Age bones found nearby on the bed of the lake, the area must have been buzzing with prehistoric life.

If, as the evidence suggests, the post-glacial lake survived almost into historical times, it leads to the question of whether there is any record or legend of the lake other than the physical archaeological story. Contemporary documentary evidence seems unlikely although considering the rich Celtic poetry and mythology associated with lakes a search in that direction is being undertaken. The Lakes of Wales have attracted fascinating folklore and myth, some, such as the Tylwyth Teg (the Welsh Fairies), are considered to be folk memories of Bronze Age peoples still surviving during the early Iron Age (cf W.J. Gruffydd, *Folklore and Myth in the Mabinogion*, University of Wales Press, 1961).

The Tylwyth Teg tended to live away from other people, often in lakes (crannogs?); they spoke a different language but occasionally one of them (the beautiful Lady of the Lake) would agree to marry a mortal on condition that the husband never touched her with iron.

Gruffydd quotes John Rhys (*Celtic Folklore,* 1901*)* on the characteristics of the Tylwyth Teg :

> The sallowness of the skin and the smallness of their stature, their dwelling underground, their dislike of iron and the comparative poverty of their homes in the matter of useful articles of furniture, their deep-rooted objection of the green sward being broken up by the plough, the success of the fairy wife in attending to the domestic animals and the dairy, the limited range generally of the fairies' ability to count; and lastly one may perhaps mention their using a language of their own which would imply a time when the little people understood no other, and explain why they should be represented doing their marketing without uttering a syllable to anybody.

Gruffydd pointed out that the Fairy Folk more often live in lakes, avoided towns, and apparently looked similar to each other – as the Chinese look to us. The fear of iron, the symbol of new invaders (?Celts) would be natural and there are many other aspects that suggest that the Tylwyth Teg preserves a folk recollection of the original inhabitants and their impact on the Celtic settlers (presumably speaking early Welsh). However, recent research is suggesting that the Welsh language is far older and was already developing before the arrival of iron.

Leland's description of Llangors Lake (1563-9) probably would have fitted the Monmouth Lake which also 'runneth into the Wy'. He wrote:

> 'The lake caullid in Walche Llin Sevathan. Here one thing is to be noted, that after a great reyne Lleveney cummeth out of the montaynes with such rage that he bringeth the color of the dark red sand with him, and ys sene by the color where he violently passeth through the mere. Thens Lleveney runneth into Wy about Glasbyry, a iii miles from Hay, the which is in the right way betwixt Hereford and Breknoc. In the lake be numbers of fish caulled in Walche cangans (?grayling, W. glasgangen) and great store of pykes, whereof many cum into Wy river. The Lake of Breknoc ons frozen over than in a thaue breking, making mervelus noise per totam viciniam. Llin Sevathan is a iiii myles by the South est from Brekenoc. It is in a bredth a mile and a ii miles in length, and where as it is deepest a xiii fathom. On the one side wel nere the ripe is a kind of weedes that goith along the Llin, wherein the spaune doth sucour, and also the great fische. At great windes the water doth surge there mervelusly. Lleveney cummeth throwgh this lake, no great river. and after a great raineis parfightly seene of a rede color in the middest of the lake...It berith as the principale fische a great number of bremes, and they appeyre in May in mightie sculles, so that sumtime they breke the large nettes; and ons frayed appereth not in the bryme of the water that yer agayn.

9

It berith also a good pikes, and perches in great numbers. Trowts also, and chevins (chubb) by cumming in of Lleveny. Menne fisch ther uniligneis and they be very narrow... Part as sum say is in the Walsche Talegarth, and part in Breknok lordship, the whiche be divided by Lleveni.'

+   +   +

Another source may be a study of field names, which of course, like so many place names in Gwent and Archenfield, are most likely to be in Welsh or have Welsh origins. Sadly, although most of the surrounding country west of the Wye remained Welsh speaking into comparatively recent times, the bowl of Monmouth was over-run by the Roman Army at an early date and then settled as a Roman industrial town which, although there was a Celtic settlement, was followed by a Norman-French fortified frontier town with a Saxon/English contribution. And so, despite the fact that even in the 18th century, it was said that as much Welsh as English was heard in Hereford and Ross-on-Wye, Monmouth seems to have remained an anglicised town.

So far, the only thing I have found that may be related to a memory of the lake is in the area of the blockage at Redbrook. There is a 'Pwl (Pwll) Mawr Wood' ('Great Pond' or 'Great Lake' or possibly 'Great Pit') running along the steep hillside above the Colman Rocks in the Wye. If the rocks are remnants of the Ice Age damming of the Wye Valley, it may be that the wood is named after the water backing upstream from the blockage; a deep pool may have remained here longer than elsewhere in the valley for there does not appear to be any pond or lake in the Pwl Mawr Wood.

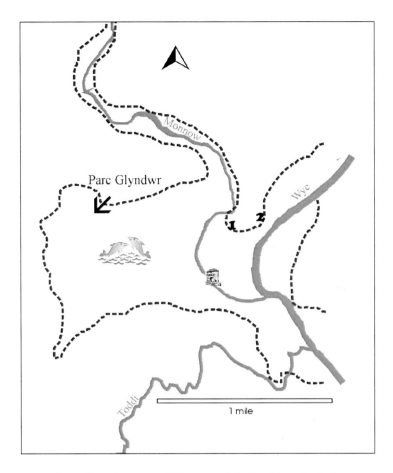

Jane Bray's map of Monmouth's Prehistoric Lake

The lake was created by a late glacial blockage of the Wye Valley in the gorge above Redbrook which pooled up an enormous body of water to reach as far as the Parc Glyndŵr development site. The water level would have been at a minimum of 23.50 metres above the Ordnance Datum – the bed of the lake at Parc Glyndŵr – which would mean that at least six metres of water would have covered much of Monmouth. Site 1 (24 Monnow Street) contained an alluvial layer with the early Bronze Age arrowhead and Site 2 similar deposits sealing a middle Stone Age camp site and late Iron Age pottery, indicating, that the lake had survived into the 1ˢᵗ century BC. Sites 1 (24 Monnow Street) and 2 (4 St James' Street) are on the sides of the 'tongue' of the gravel terraces where the Wye and the Monnow joined the lake. This may be where we should expect the rivers to deposit material they were carrying during any extensive prehistoric floods

CHAPTER ONE

A Huge Post-Glacial Lake

22-24 Monnow Street, 1999

We had reached ancient river gravels during a rescue excavation in a shop on the main street of Monmouth and while confirming that it was a natural layer Ann Leaver found a Bronze Age barbed and tanged flint arrowhead amongst the gravels.

Surely the arrowhead had to be intrusive – for the gravels were around five metres above the present river level – 21 metres above the Ordnance Datum.

However, the flint arrowhead was very unusual for it was highly polished – polished by water and sand.

Outside No. 4 St James' Street, 2011

It was a metre and a half under the road – beside an iron gas main and below the graded alluvial deposits of a primeval river bank that I noticed a fleck of black in the side of the trench. It looked like a fragment of charcoal and assuming that it had been pushed into the section by the JCB, I ran my trowel across it and scraped it away – and exposed a second fleck.

This time, I carefully lifted the tiny piece on the tip of my trowel and rubbed it between my fingers. It spread out in the distinctive soft smudge of wood charcoal.

Charcoal means fire and fire surely means humans. But this was under river gravels, some 21 metres above the Ordnance Datum, way above the present river level.

I sat down on the iron gas pipe and stared at the section.

WE were nearing the end of the ten-year-long excavation in a shop on the main street of Monmouth. For many years our archaeological society had been exploring the story of Monnow Street which was part of a very ancient route from England to western Wales. We called it the prehistoric 'A40'. The site was quite high up the street and had been occupied continuously since at least the Iron Age and included a Roman Fort and a Pre-Norman building.

Members of the public had been able to visit the under-cover excavations from the very start and thousands of people who had been to Monmouth in the 1990s may recall visiting the exhibitions and watching the work.

Ann Leaver was working towards the rear of the site and had reached what appeared to be the natural ground level of sand and pebbles – like an ancient riverbed. We assumed that it must have been millions of years since the River Wye had flowed at this height – around 21 metres above the Ordnance Datum – so it was a surprise to find that Ann was holding a small barbed and tanged flint arrowhead which she had found amongst the gravels.

It was an even greater surprise when we saw that the flint arrowhead, which was probably of early Bronze Age date, was water-worn, with highly polished surfaces.

Could the Monmouth rivers really have been flowing this high across the future town – less than 4,000 years ago? Or was there another explanation – that a giant post-glacial lake had survived for far longer than the geologists realised?

The physical evidence for a post-glacial blockage of the Wye Valley between Monmouth and Redbrook is geologically sound while the creation of a huge lake across the Monmouth flood plain is also certain, for we sit in a large bowl inside an even bigger bowl of hills; and for our three rivers there is only one way out – through the gorge. Nevertheless, Gordon McDonald's suggestion that such a lake might have survived into the late Bronze Age, or even into the Iron Age, appeared to me to be pretty unlikely until the sites in Monnow Street and St James' Street gave up their secrets.

If much of the town really was once covered by a huge lake it would have been a lake over two miles long – bigger even than Llangorse Lake – the largest in modern day southern Wales. Such a lake would have been formed from just to the north of Redbrook, where the valley closed in tightly and is today overlooked by the beautiful old church of Penallt. It would then have stretched across the alluvium of the flood plain to the Parc Glyndŵr housing site where we were to be working in 2012 to 2013.

The lake would have had a shoreline around the edge of the first or second gravel terrace and would have flooded the ground on three sides of the town and extended to the north and west, across one of the largest inland flood plains of Wales.

+   +   +

During the autumn of 2010 we began a watching brief on the replacement of gas mains around the higher parts of Monmouth and it was at the junction of St James' Street and St James' Square, with its famous old Catalpa, that we uncovered further dramatic evidence of the lost lake.

The bloomery iron slag from the small Roman iron furnaces had consistently extended to the bottom of the trench but now, as we approached St James' Square, the digging was showing that the old ground level had been rising from the west.

The trench sides were impressive, with successive deposits looking like an archaeological layered cake and at the bottom what appeared to be a river bed of graded sand and pebbles – itself lying over clean sands of an ancient flood plain. The alluvial deposit was thickening towards St James' Square – to the north-east – from where the flow must have been coming. Strangely there appeared to be little sign of humus separating the alluvial horizon from the iron slag which must have been Roman as yet we have no evidence for native iron working in the town).

I began scraping the section with a trowel to show it at its best for photography but assuming that both lower contexts were laid down long before any humans had appeared on the scene.

The black of the Roman iron slag contrasted strongly with the rounded pebbles of the supposed river bank and them in turn with the sand below. We had about half a metre to work in on each side of the iron gas main and it was in the side of the trench, near the lowest level, that I noticed the fleck of black in the sand.

+   +   +

Across Monmouth, the first and second gravel terraces or the sands of the alluvium around the two rivers were where the archaeologist's interest ended and the geologist's really began – below these lurked 'Dinosaur Country' – laid down before history began and perhaps even before modern man had appeared in Britain after a quarter of a million years of the last Ice Age. This horizon is the 'natural' – the ground not associated with humans.

I had trowelled a few centimetres of the sand when the first piece of flint appeared. There is no local flint and in any case this piece had clearly been struck by hand and may have come from as far away as Wiltshire or East Anglia.

The next few pieces of flint were flakes and one of them was burnt – evidence of a camp fire – and then I was holding a small blade less than an inch long; it had a very finely worked angled end – a 'microlith'. Microliths – the flint barbs for arrows or harpoons are one of the most distinctive artefacts of the Middle Stone Age – the *Mesolithic* – the period after the melting of the ice sheets down to the invention of farming, some thousands of years later.

The flints were examined and reported on by Elizabeth Walker, Curator with responsibility for the Palaeolithic and Mesolithic collections at the Amgueddfa Cymru – National Museum Wales in Cardiff. She reported that the assemblage was clearly Middle Stone Age – Mesolithic.

+   +   +

During the Ice Age nearly all of Wales north west of a line from Abergavenny through Orcop to Hereford was covered by massive sheets of ice but as these melted small groups of hunter-gatherers ventured across the land bridge with the Continent into what was at first a barren and treeless land. The great beasts of the earlier interglacials had died out – the elephant, woolly rhinoceros, hippopotamus, cave bear, cave lion and mammoths, which were hunted in the Wye Valley by people living in King Arthur's Cave on the Great Doward. At times King Arthur's Cave was a hyena den where these disgusting creatures dragged the remains of their kill or of their scavenging.

As the climate improved, animals and vegetation returned. At first the land was colonised by birch and pine but was later covered with coniferous forests similar to those in northern Scandinavia today. As the weather became warmer and wetter, deciduous trees such as oak, elm and alder arrived and produced dense forests across much of Britain. This also brought a new fauna.

The earliest Mesolithic peoples must have been restricted to the more open areas of the countryside in pursuit of the reindeer and elk which thrived in that environment. However, as the generations passed these were replaced by smaller prey – more 'modern' animals such as red and roe deer, wild boar, beaver, pine martin and fox. Prehistoric wild cattle – the aurochs – had survived and, although probably less dangerous than the mammoth, must have been pretty formidable creatures.

Although there is evidence of more permanent settlements, later Mesolithic camps like the one on the edge of St James' Square, were probably seasonal, for these were true hunter-gatherers – perhaps consisting of small family groups who collected wild plant food and exploited the fish and wildfowl on the banks of the Wye. Their homes, which must have been established in small forest clearings, have left few traces for they were simple affairs of thin wooden frames covered with animal skins and tree branches.

Several unusual features in the sand are perhaps best described as 'fossils' – hollows in the sand probably left by the rotting of wooden objects. One of these was perfectly straight and quite long with a number of flints lying alongside as if it were the remains of a harpoon with microlithic barbs. Another straight 'fossil' hollow was found at a right angle to the first.

A rather poignant find was part of a marine shell which must have been brought from the coast – probably as a bead on a necklace – a decoration found as early as Palaeolithic times.

It is known that our hunter-gatherer ancestors used boats and that they were active on the coasts and on inland riverbanks although forays into the forests were also made. We have found microliths before, as occasional discoveries beneath the archaeology along the flood plain in Monnow Street. However, we had no firm evidence that hunters were doing more than just passing through, losing flints during fishing or ambushing the birds and animals on the riversides.

The previous evidence for a campsite included a collection of small Mesolithic style blades found by Dave Pritchard while field-walking in Graham Long's Troy Meadow; but in that case ploughing had destroyed any evidence of a camp.

Forays into the local countryside are recorded in our area by occasional microliths well away from the rivers; for example, they hunted and may have camped on the Buckholt Hill where we have discovered microliths and flint flakes in and around an area overlooking the two river valleys. There appear to have been a number of similar sites on hillsides around Skenfrith.

The Monmouth hunter-gatherers' settlement was situated on the banks of the post-glacial lake which, with the influx of the flooded rivers, had covered the shores with a layer of pebbles and sand which today lie a metre below modern St James' Street and seals the prehistoric remains.

Although some hunter-gatherer camps have been found to be about 25 metres across we recovered similar flints in early river sands in nearby Wyebridge Street. Perhaps this shows that our camp was very large or, perhaps more likely, that there was more than one Stone Age site on the banks of the lake. The campers may have returned for millennia for Monmouth must have been a good site – between three river valleys.

+   +   +

Late in the mitigation work there was a crucially important discovery related to the great lake and the history of Monmouth. Towards the surface of the sand but definitely sealed beneath the pebbly 'riverbank', was a small sherd of late Iron Age pottery.

A sherd of Iron Age pot was a surprise and, just then, something of a disappointment, because of course it meant that our Stone Age camp site was not in a closed Stone Age context.

The true importance of the find was to sink in later, for the discovery at first appeared to show (as did the water polished flint arrowhead from the other side of town) that the Wye was flowing above the 21 metre contour in St James' Street at that time – a ridiculous idea!

Of course, there was another explanation – the survival of the prehistoric lake. But – into the late Iron Age?

Dr Peter Webster had examined the potsherd which he considered to be native calcite gritted ware – typical of products of the late Iron Age and early Roman periods in South Wales – dating from around 200BC to AD50. However, as the sherd was decorated with horizontal grooving, he felt that it was more likely to be Iron Age rather than Roman, which were normally undecorated.

This dating was supported when we sent charcoal from the same layer of sand to the Scottish Universities Radiocarbon Research Centre and later received a date of c100BC and 40BC (*Appendix*). This was a similar date to that suggested by Peter Webster and can be seen as good evidence that if the bank of sand and pebbles were the edge of the lake, then the lake had survived until sometime around 100BC – at least. There was to be further evidence of the survival of the lake at Parc Glyndŵr.

So, once upon a time both St James' Street and Monnow Street – both sides of the upper town – had contained pebbly lakeside banks on the shores of an enormous post-glacial lake. The evidence not only supported the existence of the 'McDonald' lake but appears to show that it had survived even later than Gordon McDonald himself had thought – into the late Iron Age. He told me that he had believed that the lake had disappeared during the massive floods of the 3rd and 4th centuries BC when floodwater should have finally eroded away the bar at Redbrook. However, he commented: 'The only way the demise of the lake can be accurately plotted is to follow the archaeology.' We all agreed that it must have gone by the time the Romans arrived.

McDonald did not think the lake vanished overnight but could have drained over a more extended period (with some fluctuation during flood events). If the archaeology is dateable and datum heights can be plotted it should be possible to plot the timeline of the retreating waterfront.

+   +   +

We had seen the proof that the horrendous floods of the 14th century AD had reached the site at 24 Monnow Street and came close to it in 1947, while in 1963 water from the Monnow was witnessed rushing out into Monnow Street from Nailer's Lane. On the other hand, the water of the lake would have been lapping around the edge of Agincourt Square

There is ample evidence that the lake had drained by Roman times, with occupations and iron working on the banks of the Wye and at

Overmonnow (in areas which presumably would have previously been under water). There is native pottery from Overmonnow too – once again it's late Iron Age/early Roman. There is also Iron Age pottery from 24 Monnow Street, including briquette from the salt industry at Droitwich and there's also the Roman fort front ditch there in the AD50s, so the lake must have gone by then. The late Ice Age blockage of the Wye Valley, the reason for the post-glacial lake and its survival, was the existence of the Wye Gorge below Monmouth. Here the valley closes significantly and at its narrowest point the debris from the melting glacier would have accumulated sufficiently create the lake.

The location of the obstruction seems to be marked by the Colman Rocks in the bed of the Wye and by a presumed moraine on the Welsh bank of the river (SO 53312 10382).

There are no similar features to these – the rocks or the presumed moraine – in this part of the Wye Valley.

If upper Monnow Street and St James' Street had been the shores of a prehistoric lake, its waters would have covered the alluvium across the flood plains to an opposite shore on the first and second gravel terraces – overlooked by Parc Glyndŵr – a kilometre away.

Gordon McDonald had previously noted that during the 4th century BC climatic deterioration occurred across Europe and at that time Lake Constance, at the head of the Rhine, has been estimated at 30 feet above the present level.

Sustained Continent-wide precipitation of this magnitude could well have seen epic flooding across the whole of the River Wye catchment area, possibly eroding away some of the geology around Redbrook, primarily responsible for damming the now drained Monmouth basin.

We have seen the edges of existing lakes, with their thin beaches, where the wind separates the sand from the pebbles with a motion which polishes the small stones – and perhaps a Bronze Age arrowhead. It may have polished them as efficiently as the waves along the seashore would have done. And of course, the entry into the lake of the two rivers around the higher ground at the top of Monmouth – specially the Wye in flood – would surely have caused them to drop the larger material that they were carrying.

There were other things in the past which were strange. One instance of which I recall was many years ago while field walking the plough soil on Graham Long's Troy Meadow with Dave Pritchard. We had found scores of flints, including Mesolithic and Neolithic ones; they were scattered across the fields when Dave commented: "It's strange – all the flints seem to be above the 60ft contour."

+   +   +

I attempted to disprove the extraordinary evidence that the lake had survived into the late Iron Age. The best evidence at first seemed to be a saddle quern-stone, for grinding corn with a roller, which I had found on top of the backfill of a drainage trench during the construction of Clawdd Du housing estate, Overmonnow, in the 1960s.

Overmonnow was built on the Monmouth alluvium – still a flood area today – and would have been at least 6 metres under the water of the prehistoric lake. Saddle querns are found amongst the remains left by the earliest farmers in the New Stone Age but they were still being used in late Iron Age and early Roman times. Therefore we must assume that, if the lake had survived almost into historic times the people grinding corn in Overmonnow had moved onto the rich pastureland left by the draining of the lake during the late Iron Age. We have also found native pottery of the period on the same estate less than a hundred yards away.

+   +   +

Wondering if there was access to the sea from the great lake I discussed it with Gordon McDonald who e-mailed me:

Circa 2000BC, for a couple of hundred years, and again from 1100BC for a similar period, sea level was higher than today – between 1 and 2 metres higher, during cycles of what we know today as Global Warming. Winding back post-glacial rebound, some 2mm uplift per year (2m per 1000 years), around 2000BC land levels in the Wye valley would have been 8 metres lower than they are today and one thousand years later land levels would be 6 metres lower than they are today.

So circa 2000BC, the highest spring tides in the Wye would have been some 10 metres above their present level which means that twice a month at Redbrook the tides would reach the present day 20m contour (2+8+10*=20m) 10* metres OD is the height to which the highest Spring Tides reach in the Bristol Channel.

Around 1000BC the highest spring tides in the Wye would have been some 8 metres above their present level, so again twice a month at Redbrook the tides would peak at around the present day 18m contour (2+6+10=18m).

In the mid 2nd millennium BC sea level fell but during that time, and again as the climate began to deteriorate at the end of the Bronze Age, it would still be possible to float up and down river from the lake to the sea and back.

Gordon has rounded the figures above to whole numbers for easier reading.

On the question of the Overmonnow saddle quern, Gordon commented:

During the mid to late 1st millennium BC sea level fell dramatically, possibly by as much as +7 metres but by circa AD100 sea level had advanced again to its higher level - circa some 2 metres above its current level. However, with land levels only 4 metres lower than today the high spring tides would only be peaking at the present day 16m contour (2+4+10=16m). At the time Julius Caesar crossed to Britain circa 53BC sea level would have been rising but only equated to today's level so the spring tides in Monmouth would only be peaking at around the present day 14m (4+10=14m) contour. So in the late Iron Age and early Roman period, the severe rainfall and river flooding of three hundred years earlier would have subsided, leaving Over-Monnow vulnerable to floods on more or less the same scale as it is today. For much of the time this area would have been quite habitable.

He later added:

With regard to sea level calculations obviously it's not an exact science so I have set out below the sort of thing you may find useful as explanation.

For navigation purposes tidal levels in the upper Bristol Channel are calculated annually for both Avonmouth and Sharpness Docks with daily details published in the Admiralty Tide Tables. The highest Spring Tides in the Bristol Channel currently peak at around 9.5 metres Ordnance Datum but on occasion given certain conditions such as low air pressure and extreme wind velocity can result in tidal surges which exceed this level by a significant margin.

Geological uplift has been a feature of the lower Wye valley and to a lesser extent the Severn valley over an extended period of geological time but generally over the last 10,000 years there has been a major influence due to Post Glacial Rebound. Winding back this geological uplift to, for example, the end of the Neolithic, 4000 years ago, at Monmouth would see land levels between six and eight metres lower than they are today, while 3,000 years ago the calculation is four to six metres lower and 2,000 years ago two to four metres lower.

For the last six thousand years it has been possible to track changing climate as cycles of Global Warming and Cooling, each cycle period being approximately one thousand years, with warm climatic interludes around the turn of each millennium and distinctly cooler interludes in the middle of each millennium. Sea levels have reacted very strongly to these changes in climate with at the turn of each millennium sea levels showing a distinct rise, while in the middle of each millennium regressing to a much lower level. These changes in sea level can be quite dramatic with for instance a roughly 8 metre rise in sea level recorded between 400BC and AD100.

Taking the known tidal maximum for the Upper Bristol Channel, winding back Post Glacial Rebound and applying appropriate calculations for past sea level it is possible to estimate against present day Ordnance Datum land contours the height to which the tidal peaks could have reached at specific times in the past. For instance circa 2000BC it is very likely that the highest Spring Tides in the Monmouth Basin could have peaked very close to the present day 20 metre contour. Circa 1000BC the twice monthly Spring Tides could have reached the 18 metre contour and when the Romans arrived the Wye would have been sufficiently tidal to permit access by the largest seagoing transport ships.

It soon became apparent that there had been considerable Bronze Age activity on the Gravel Terraces overlooking the lake at Parc Glyndŵr; that was a kilometre away from today's Monmouth town centre and over two miles from the site of the presumed blockage above Redbrook.

The surprise that the great lake had survived for so long was followed by another surprise – there were strange remains overlooking the lake.

The water-worn Bronze Age arrowhead came from these ancient gravels
Scales: Flint arrowhead 1 Centimetre (Photograph Jane Bray); Ranging pole in feet

The gas main replacement watching brief in 2011

The St James' Street gas mains section: The dark layer of iron slag in the middle of the section contained Roman pottery and lies directly above the pebbles and sand of the alluvial deposit which itself seals the sand at the bottom of the section. The worked flints and other finds from the Mesolithic camp site came from the sand layer at the bottom of the section as did the sherd of late Iron Age pottery and two associated radio-carbon dates. Photograph: Denis Loffhagen

Peter Bere's reconstruction of the Middle Stone Age camp

2 cm

Microliths and other flints from the hunter gatherers' camp site.
Identified by Dr Elizabeth Walker.   Photograph by Denis Loffhagen

*The lake shore of graded pebbles and sand covering the silty sand which
produced the Middle Stone Age flints and the Iron Age potsherd*
Photograph: Denis Loffhagen

*An Iron Age cooking pot rim sherd from the shore of the lake at
24 Monnow Street, it is similar to one found below the alluvial
deposit in St James' Street*
Scale Cms. Identified by Dr Peter Webster.   Photograph: Denis Loffhagen

Labels on image: White Hill, Parc Glyndŵr, Gibraltar Hill, Drybridge House, Monnow Bridge, **Monmouth**, Chippenham, Monnow River, A40, River Trothy, Breakthrough of glacial lake, Wye Bridge, **PENALLT**, rook Valley, River Wye, River Wye

Peter Bere's reconstruction of the Monmouth Pleistocene Lake.
The lake survived until sometime in the 1st century BC. The melt water had been
held up by debris in the gorge between Redbrook and Monmouth creating the
huge post-glacial lake which filled the Monmouth Basin.

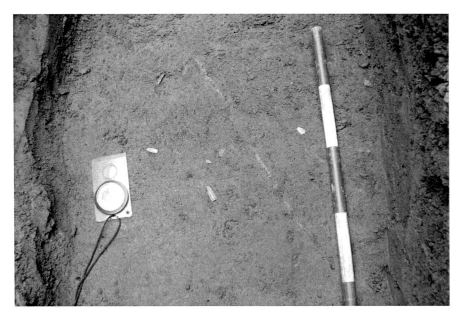

St James Street hunter gatherers' camp site. Linear void and microliths resembling a rotted wooden shaft and flint barbs. Could this be the 'ghost' of a harpoon lost in the water on the edge of the lake?

Parc Glyndŵr. Gravel beds of the post-glacial lake at the water table

The Colman Rocks, looking east

The Colman Rocks, looking north

The Colman presumed moraine is just beyond the trees

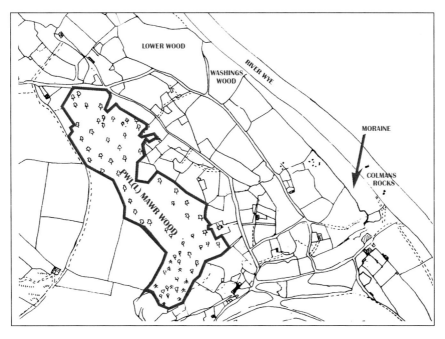

Pwl (Pwll) Mawr Wood ('The Great Pond, Lake or Pit') overlooking the post-glacial blockage of the Wye Valley above Redbrook

CHAPTER TWO

An Ancient Lagoon

In 2010, before beginning the Parc Glyndŵr housing project on the edge of Monmouth, the developers had a large drainage channel excavated on three sides of the site – to the north, the east and the west.

The results of the digging caused considerable interest around the adjoining estates for it exposed up to a metre of black peat together with layers of anaerobic clay which must have formed over long periods under water or in very wet conditions.

I saw the excavations and assumed that the copse of trees beside the thickest of the peat marked the centre of an ancient lake; we later found that it marked a lagoon which was left when the post-glacial lake had drained.

I HAD been digging for over half a century and had been thinking of retiring – well, at least of becoming an amateur again. But there was no way that I was going to miss this, so our small professional unit, *Monmouth Archaeology,* put in a tender to become the archaeological contractors. The developers, Charles Church Wales, accepted our tender and we became the archaeologists on what soon proved to be a unique site and one which I later realised should be of international interest.

We worked well with the developers and their sub-contractors, Randalls, while the management showed interest and gave us their support and encouragement – especially when it came to paying for radiocarbon dating.

It appeared at first that the deeper parts of the lake were marked by the peat exposed in the western drainage ditch and centred on the copse of trees on the western side of the development. The peat, of varying thicknesses, extended halfway across the site.

We did not realise then that the peat marked a lagoon that was presumably created when the main post-glacial lake drained away.

The original gravely bed of the lake had covered much of the development site but with a shoreline running along the south-eastern side. This was to be where the prehistoric sites were revealed – just above the surface of the lake.

The stratification in the lagoon began immediately above the accumulated gravels and pebbles of the thick beds of the post-glacial lake (the last to be dated to the Iron Age) with a layer of white lime marl which was produced by pondweed (*Potamogeton* species). This must have marked the quiet waters of the new lagoon.

The silting up of the lagoon presumably then progressed to the swamp and marsh phases, producing the peat deposits (with a Roman date). The constantly waterlogged conditions then created a layer of anaerobic clay (gley), also with a Roman date, which was succeeded by a red-brown clay and then the boggy topsoil.

As a schoolboy I recall that the field remained a reedy marshland with scattered ponds and willow trees until the farmer filled in the ponds and drained the field, this was sometime during the second half of the 20th century.

+   +   +

This is probably the appropriate place to say something about the background to the site. This is the land of the medieval Bailey Pit which is situated below the eastern slopes of the White Hill, overlooking Monmouth's extensive flood plain. It was once one of three Bailey Pit farms but the other two now lie ruined under brambles on the edges of the woodland, together with two other farms and various cottages deeper in the forest. There were also two Roman Forts on the eastern shoulder of the hill overlooking Monmouth which was the Roman town of Blestium – and with westward views across the plain of Gwent, towards the Roman fortress of Usk and the Black Mountains beyond.

The field of the development (of 85 houses) was always boggy, with kingcups, yellow flag and bullrushes and was one of our haunts as children; here we collected frogs and newts and, if one's parents had not discouraged it, went birds' egg collecting. We searched for the nests of curlews, wagtails and lapwings (we called them peewits, of course). Sometimes an otter came up the brook and we often saw kingfishers flashing along the stream and dragonflies hunting on the wing. The last otter I ever saw was killed by Mr Jackson with a spade in nearby Watery Lane and I've not seen curlews or kingfishers here for many years although the bullrushes and flag (yellow irises to us), frogs and newts have survived and have taken over the banks of the new flood attenuation pond.

Together with the Rockfield 'new town' and Overmonnow, the site of Parc Glyndŵr sits in the four kilometre long bowl which is bordered by hills from Croft-y-Bwla, off the Rockfield Road, around to Gibraltar Hill, above Monmouth's suburb of Overmonnow. Centrally the bowl is dominated by the 600 feet high White Hill on the west while rainfall from the bowl is taken to the River Monnow by two small brooks – the Wonastow Road brook, which doesn't appear to have a name, and the Scud brook which borders Watery Lane.

During and after the Battle of Britain in World War II the Ministry of Defence looked at the fields of the Bailey Pitt as a possible landing site for aircraft at a time when they were hiding Spitfires at Chepstow Racecourse. Several local boys from the council estate went out into the fields here and talked to the men who were probing the ground and who told them what they were doing – checking the ground for the possible building of an airstrip – presumably because it was one of the larger level areas in the region. The men were obviously not concerned that the lads might have been German spies, although it is more likely they realised that a bog was no place to land an aeroplane.

Cyril Ward was then the farmer, having taken over the Bailey Pitt in 1940. Mr Ward was interviewed for the *Farming Reporter* magazine in November 1954, No 54 (I am grateful to Charles Ward for supplying a copy of the magazine). After discussing the famous ghosts of Bailey Pit and the 'old skeletons of cattle which had been left to rot in the wood above the farm, near the Offa's Dyke Path' (not Offa's Dyke – that is on the other side of the Wye) the *Reporter* went on to discuss Mr Ward ('Ferguson Farmer – No 17') and the farm:

Cyril Ward was born and bred on Wheatfields Estate, below the present farm, and he had known Bailey Pit as a cold, wet farm all his life. He realised it would require extensive drainage work to get the water, that deadly enemy of low land, away. He tackled first an eight and a half acre bog which had broken the spirit of previous farmers and drained it successfully.

We were soon to discover evidence of Mr Ward's drainage work – scores of drains of all sorts – large, small and U-shaped ceramic ones, plastic ones and trenches filled with gravel or industrial slag and 'mole' machine driven ones.

The 'bog' was probably in the same area of the ancient lagoon – land of the appropriately named 'Bailey Pit' or – as in early times – 'Cadeput'. As 'cad' is the Welsh word for a 'battle', might it not refer to something else, the memory of which has been lost in these damp and misty fields?

+   +   +

The peat was too soft for building on so it had to be removed to be mixed with the overlying clays. Fortuitously the two were, at first, removed separately which gave us the chance to examine the layers more thoroughly than would otherwise have been possible; this was essential with the surfaces of several clays and when the bottom of the peat was exposed.

A flat bucket was used on the machine for a toothed bucket would have proved disastrous in understanding the stratification or for seeing any features in the various stages of the silting and demise of the lake. The flat buckets gave us the chance to recognise, although not necessarily to understand, some remarkable remains, at first during the excavations for the foundations of the main roadways, which runs east to west towards the centre of the lake, and later on the land which would have overlooked the lake from the south.

+   +   +

It was an appalling day in the wet spring of 2012. I reached into my fluorescent overcoat pocket for a plastic bag and found a pocketful of muddy water. Cold rain had been lashing down for the best part of a week and Parc Glyndŵr was in a horrendous condition – one old hand told me that he had not seen a site like it in over forty years.

It appears that the best way to make it rain is to declare a drought, which is what had been done across much of southern Britain during the Spring. The announcements were soon followed by prolonged and record downpours and of course, floods; and there was worse to come during the following winter.

The contractors were removing the peat before constructing the first of the estate roads and this meant peeling off the surface red clay which was covered in the thin reed-grown topsoil. Below the red clay was the grey anaerobic 'gley'– the clay formed under water or under prolonged wet and oxygen-free conditions. This lay directly over the layer of peat.

The removal of the peat revealed the white layer of lime of a sort which we had never encountered before. It reacted strongly with dilute hydrochloric acid and looked like lime which was deposited on the fields during farming, even though there was no way that it could have been dumped there during recent times – why spread lime on a marsh in any case? In *Soils for the Archaeologist* by I. W. Cornwall, we found that it was produced by pondweed of the *Potamogeton* family and is called marl – I call it pondweed marl or lime marl to distinguish it from other marls. Peter Bere has sampled the deposit from beneath the peat and his microscopic examination showed that the grains were identical to gypsum.

The peat varied in thickness, thinning to the east, but there was just about a metre of it in the western side of the drainage channel previously dug around the perimeter of the site.

How old was the peat? We had no idea. Most environmental studies suggested that peat was laid down at about 0.5mm per year which would mean that ours, at the thickest, should have taken around 2,000 years to accumulate; however, the peat had been superseded by the gley and then by the clay and topsoil so it could be considerably older.

The next obvious question was, of course, how quickly the pondweed marl took to accumulate underneath the peat and that's a question I can still find no-one to answer, including the experts at Kew.

+ + +

I was soon reduced to wearing an old army cape– of the type seen in the black and white horror film archives of the First World War (with a fluorescent jacket pinned to the outside).

Although keen to move on and fill the excavation with hard-core and concrete, the builders held back while I collected samples and studied the ground. These were the most miserable conditions I had experienced and the digger-driver, in his heated cab, fully deserved the banter he received.

It appeared that nothing much had been preserved in the peat, or in the underlying marl so in the beginning the watching brief on the lake remains was disappointing. Especially as there was a total absence of votive offerings, as found in other Welsh or Irish lakes and bogs, not even boring soggy timbers were preserved, as at Flag Fen.

+ + +

Dating is confusing for it was on the surface of the gley that I had noticed a scatter of charcoal near the edge of the peat and presumably the side of the lake. As I was collecting samples of the scatter of charcoal I found a rounded flint scraper amongst it.

The scraper had been made from a fragment of a broken Neolithic polished flint axe. The Neolithic – the New Stone Age – is dated to sometime between 4000BC and 2200BC, so the piece had to have originally been at least some 4,000 years old.

However, a radiocarbon date from the charcoal came out as Iron Age, 490BC (*Appendix B*). The anomaly was partially explained when Elizabeth Walker identified the re-working as Bronze Age. Another flint from the clay near the central roadway is likely to be earlier for it appears to be part of a Mesolithic blade.

+　　+　　+

Although nothing much seemed to have been preserved in the acid peat, finds did include a small group of bones and some wood from the bed of the south-eastern part of the lake. They are described later, one of them produced a radiocarbon date in the Iron Age, c525BC (*Appendix B*).

One of the interesting features on the bed of the lake was what must have been its shore line overlooked by the prehistoric remains described in Chapters Three and Five. It was first revealed close to the eastern side of the copse. The surface of the bed of the lake here is composed of finely settled small pebbles beneath the pondweed marl and giving the appearance of a carefully set floor. It was on this surface that the few bones to have survived were found (horse, sheep and cow) and were kindly examined by Felicity Taylor (Monmouth) and Rose Davis (Trinity Saint David University). The bones constitute Iron Age domestic waste and are the best evidence of a settlement on or near the site during that period. Rose Davis' report is included in Chapter 10.

The same vicinity was remarkably rich in spreads of the pondweed marl which contained, in a small area, many thousands of snail shells (close to the edge of the lake); very few snail shells were found in the marl elsewhere except in the deposits around Building Plot 52, which must also have been a shoreline. It seems likely that at the time the pondweed was mostly living along the shores of the later lake or lagoon and that the marl marked shallower water. Areas of absence or a variation in the thickness of the pondweed marl which occurred across the site may be an indication of the depth of the water – especially if was too deep for the pondweed roots to reach the bottom.

+　　+　　+

As this book was at the proof stage (late August 2013) a small stream channel was revealed crossing Plot 43 and cut into the bed of the post-glacial lake. The stream was running southwards and cutting the peat; it containied several deposits. The lower sediments, included silt and sand which produced a dozen lumps of bloomery iron slag with fire clay. A C14 date has been commissioned using charcoal from the same context.

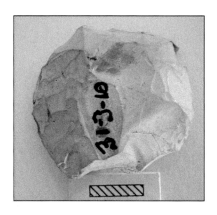

*A Bronze Age flint thumb scraper made from a fragment of a
New Stone Age polished axe.   From the lakeside at Parc Glyndŵr.*

Photograph by Jane Bray; Identification by Dr Elizabeth Walker

Parc Glyndŵr.   Examining the peat in the drainage channel in 2010

The Parc Glyndŵr development (west at top)   Photograph by John Sorrell

Peat below the anaerobic clay (gley)

PREHISTORIC FEATURES

SHORE OF POST-GLACIAL LAKE AND LAGOON

RESIDULE LAGOON

RIVER MONNOW

POST-GLACIAL LAKE

DERN DITCH

'ROX. EXTENT OF LAGOON

Parc Glyndŵr, with the post-glacial lake covering most of the site and the edges
of the residual 'lagoon' marked   Photograph by John Sorrell

Plot 43. The stream bed is cutting the lagoon deposits and into the bed of the post-glacial lake. The iron slag came from the tip of the ranging pole.

Plot 43. Bloomery iron slag with fireclay - from the bottom of the stream bed cutting the stratification of the lagoon

CHAPTER THREE

The Burnt Mounds

Many Bronze Age burnt mounds (drifts of fired stones and pebbles) are Scheduled Ancient Monuments with one of the more famous being that at Rotherwas, near Hereford (The Serpentine Way) which was the cause of considerable controversy when the remains were due to be covered up and preserved in situ. During a very lively Hereford City Council planning meeting a number of elderly protesters were arrested by the Police.

BURNT MOUNDS are distinctive features which typically date to the Bronze Age although a few have been attributed to the Iron Age and Roman periods. They have especially survived in the uplands of Britain, Europe and in Ireland, where they are known as 'fulacht fiadh'. These mounds consist of fire-cracked stones and fragments of charcoal which have been discarded after use and slowly built up to form a mound.

All the burnt mounds discovered so far have been close to a water source which would seem to be integral to the use of such sites. Usually, there is an adjacent hearth and trough, which may have been lined with wood or clay to provide a watertight seal. Discussion as to the function of these sites still reigns. As yet no conclusive evidence has been found, but the assumption is that stones (pot-boilers) were heated in a hearth and then dropped into water held in the trough. There would need to be a good supply of wood available to fuel the fires. This would not have presented a problem for apparently most of the land was covered in forest until Saxon times and a supply of pebbles or stones were usually within easy reach, in this case on the slopes of the White Hill – not around the lake.

Conventionally, burnt mounds were thought to be cooking sites although often very little bone has been found. The absence of bone in Monmouth (unless burnt) is easily explained by its poor survival in acid soil but this explanation is not entirely adequate elsewhere for it seems to be equally rare on sites where soil conditions are favourable for its preservation. This calls into question the traditional interpretation that all burnt mounds are cooking sites. Other theories range from fulling, leather or textile production to making beer. There is also the theory that the aim was to produce steam, by dropping the heated stones in water, to create saunas or bending wood when constructing boats, which may have relevance to the Parc Glyndŵr site. Many of these theories seem equally viable and there is no reason to suppose the sites were limited to one specific purpose, indeed they may have been multi-purpose sites. It may even be that this was an annual activity which was carried out during the drier seasons of spring or summer with such industries as wool processing (fulling) or during seasonal hunting trips.

There is often a scarcity of artefacts and debris which would be associated with a more permanent occupation or settlement. Many of the sites consist of successive accumulations of burnt stones indicating that they were something more than unique visits. The Parc Glyndŵr burnt mounds which were spread around the area of the attenuation pond over a long period of time may support that interpretation.

+   +   +

Four burnt mounds were revealed during the excavation of the attenuation pond; these were especially clustered on the south-western side of the pond at slightly varying levels and producing different radiocarbon dates. A fifth burnt mound was exposed during the excavation of the drainage ditch immediately outside the western boundary of the development and another one during the digging of a house foundation trench in Plot 71 to the north. Both of these were again close to the edge of the lake and lagoon.

Burnt stones, indicating a seventh example, were found during the extension of the excavation to explore the westward continuation of the linear channels cutting across Burnt Mound 3. All the burnt mounds along the edge of the attenuation pond were within an area 30m long. This is quite a large concentration of activity but as the mounds were not huge and were rather scattered it could indicate seasonal visits; the horizon of the mounds, being so similar to that of the lake, probably supports the idea that the site would have been increasingly wet and probably flooded during the winter.

No trenches or 'troughs', which are often associated with burnt mounds, were uncovered although an irregular pit did exist near the centre of the mound which contained large amounts of charcoal, including some pieces up to 0.30m long. Heavy charcoal was also a feature on some parts of the mound.

We recovered more than a dozen sherds of decorated Bronze Age pottery from amongst the burnt stones but the flint flakes appeared to be mostly confined to the channels where they were easier to see against the clay background. It seems likely that many small flakes would have gone undetected amongst the burnt stones and charcoal of the burnt mound.

All the pottery sherds are very soft and quite coarse, they are organic-tempered with chaff or possibly dung. There are rare quartz grains up to 0.5mm across in the fabric while the scarcity of mica may indicate (although unlikely) a non-local origin. The sherds are thought to be of early Bronze Age date when pottery types and decoration were diverse and intricate with elaborate geometric designs and motifs. The small assemblage may represent one or more pots, probably food vessels. The sherds are stab decorated and one piece bears part of a cordon or collared rim.

Collared urns are jars with wide, thick rims often distinct from the vessel's body. Most examples are fairly large and some can be up to 500mm high, but smaller examples, which can be held comfortably in one hand, were also made. The rims are usually straight and leaning inwards. They can be decorated and may have an internal bevel. Common decoration styles include cord, incised, fingernail or impressed, in a variety of patterns such as, for example, chevrons, herring-bone or in-filled triangles. This type appears around 2200BC continuing until at least 1200BC and is common throughout Britain and Ireland. These are mainly found in funerary contexts (hence the name 'urn') and often found upside-down over cremated bones. This may not have been their primary function but examples in domestic contexts rarely survive.

Cordoned urns have some similarities with the collared urn (the vessel size and overall shape). Cordoned urns have quite simple rims with raised cordons running around the girth and perhaps lower down. The cordons divide up the area of the vessel to create bipartite or tripartite spaces, depending on the cordons present. The styles of decoration and techniques are also similar to the Collared urn, although often the Cordoned urn is less elaborately decorated. Cordoned urns are common in the north of Britain and continued to be made into the first millennium BC.

Food vessels are squat jars often with decorated bevelled rims and decoration over the body, sometimes from the rim to the base. As the name suggests, the assumption is that these were used to hold or cook food, as opposed to drink. There are three sub-classes of food vessel, termed simple, bipartite and tripartite, based on the design of the body and often each part is delineated by a raised cordon or carination. This type is very common in the north.

Jane Bray

+   +   +

Although there was considerable activity on the banks of the lake from the New Stone Age to the Iron Age, there are few prehistoric monuments in the surrounding area. Bronze Age monuments, which one might have expected near the lake, are notably absent from the whole of the Monmouth bowl – the nearest ones being the three Harold Stones at Trellech, the Marion's Stone, near Staunton, and the Queen Stone on the flood plain at Huntsham, near Goodrich. Perhaps centuries of intensive farming has removed other similar monuments.

However, prehistoric flints and stone axes have been found during ploughing all around Monmouth, with Bronze Age axes at Penallt, Trellech and Dingestow.

Potamogeton pond weed which deposits lime marl on the bed of the 'lagoon'

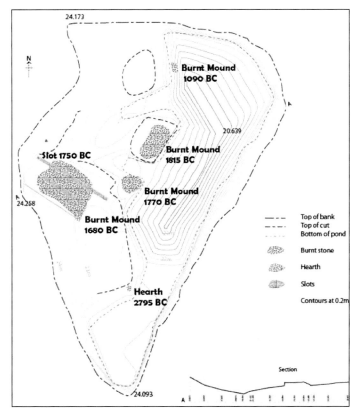

Dr Neil Phillips' plan of the prehistoric sites revealed during the excavation of the attenuation pond. The site of the ancient lake is nearby – to the north and west. The contours are those created during the machine excavations. Other burnt mounds were later found outside the area of the pond.

Fired stones on Burnt Mound 3

Burnt Mound 3 crossed by the channels filled with anaerobic clay

The Parc Glyndŵr decorated Bronze Age pottery.
Top left: cordoned or collared rim with stabbed decoration.
Top right: base sherd.   Bottom row: stab-decorated body sherds

Stripping of the clay and peat to expose the pondweed lime marl

CHAPTER FOUR

The Vanished River

Peat only forms in waterlogged, possibly stagnant, lagoons and that would not necessarily be the conditions around most of Monmouth's post-glacial lake where there was a wave-formed beach and an active flow of water. If the level of the lake, for one reason or another, dropped for an extended period, leaving a partially flooded inlet or lagoon (as seems to have been the case in part of Parc Glyndŵr) then peat would have rapidly formed. As the lake level finally fell – probably in the late Iron Age – it must have produced the peat layer with its Roman period radiocarbon date. Gordon McDonald

DURING the stripping of the peat in Plots 60 to 64, near the centre of the new estate, in October 2012, the north-eastern shore of the lagoon was exposed, together with a spread of compacted alluvial sands and gravels which were probably the bed of the original post-glacial lake. What appears to have been the bank of a river, feeding into the lake, was some two metres out from the eastern section of the excavation – running in a north-easterly to south-westerly direction – towards the deepest part of the lagoon.

The alluvial deposits consisted up to 0.50m thick clean coarse sand with layers and lenses of graded rounded pebbles and gravels. The consolidated small pebbles of the bed of the lake pre-dated these deposits and extended over all of the excavated area; this was lying over larger pebbles of the lake bed (up to some 0.10m across). The sand and various grades of pebbles often appeared as lenses inside the thick layers of other material – especially in the 'riverside' parts.

The pondweed marl did not extend for more than halfway up the excavated area, with a thin layer of it lying over the pebbles and sand immediately below the peat. The river appears to have vanished rather rapidly to become a swamp or marsh.

A large area of the peat and its overlying clay and topsoil had been removed in the 20th century – possibly during the middle of the century. Fragments of china and stoneware were included in the fill. I have been unable to trace precisely when this happened although it must have been during the ownership by the Ward family

Resumé: The Great Lake and the Missing River

A glacial dam of the Wye Valley at Redbrook caused the formation of a huge lake which stretched back from the blockage to around the Parc Glyndŵr site off Watery Lane/Rockfield Road. The lake was fed by the three Monmouth Rivers – The Wye, the Monnow and the Troddi (Trothy), of which it would have been the Monnow which entered the lake on the Parc Glyndŵr site.

Prehistoric alluvial deposits in Monmouth appeared to show the depth of the lake to have been over 21 metres above the Ordnance Survey Datum. The bed of the lake at Parc Glyndŵr is consistently around 23m OD or a little more above the Datum. This would mean that all of Overmonnow and much of Monmouth, up to Agincourt Square, would have been under water, giving sufficient depth to have deposited the sand and pebbles in Monnow Street and St James Street. The suggestion that the lake still existed into the Iron Age is supported at Parc Glyndŵr by radiocarbon dates from bone and wood recovered from the bottom of the lake near its southern shore. Equally significant is the late Iron Age potsherd (with a wide date range of c.200BC to AD200) and radiocarbon dates from beneath the alluvial deposits in St James Square (c100BC and c40BC).

At least part of the lake had passed the swamp stage by Roman times for a radiocarbon date (cAD195) from a sample of peat from the western modern drainage channel. The drain had cut through the thickest deposit of the peat – just to the west of the development site – the date is supported by a sherd of Samian ware attributed to AD140 to AD200 found in the anaerobic clay over the top of the peat in the north-western part of the same western drainage channel.

The River Monnow seems to have joined the lake from the north-east where it deposited banks of sand, gravel and pebbles along a line corresponding to the eastern half of Parc Glyndŵr Plots 60 to 64 and pointing towards the deepest concentration of the peat. The grain sizes of the sand shows that this was a flowing stream where grains were dominantly 0.5mm in size – most of the smaller grains staying in suspension to be carried on downstream. The associated gravels and pebbles of the lake bed increase in size with depth, up to and beyond 10cm across; they spread across the whole of the excavated area of the four plots while the coarse sand and lesser gravels and pebbles are restricted to around 2m out from the south-eastern section; this shows the apparent direction of the stream at that time.

Consequently, the suggestion is that an ancient post-glacial lake, fed by the three rivers, survived almost into historic times to be replaced by a still or very slow-moving lagoon.

During the life of the lake, the fast-moving River Monnow (and the other rivers) feeding the lake would have created movement which deterred the extensive growth of vegetation along the lake shores – a process which would have been accentuated by occasional floods.

There are indications of rising water levels which extended beyond the margins of the lake and gathered together thousands of terrestrial snails which are occasionally preserved in the pondweed marl along the lines of the shore or close to it. Regular flooding outside the lake is shown by the rising ground produced by settled silt above the Bronze Age levels.

It is not known how long it would have taken to completely drain the Monmouth basin or what routes the three rivers would then have travelled when the lake finally broke through the blockage of the valley above Redbrook. The Wye probably took a similar course to that of today while the Monnow may have wandered across the flood plain in a large loop, passing over the Parc Glyndŵr site to somewhere in the area of Drybridge Park to join the Wye in the region it does today. What appear to have been the alluvial sands and pebbles of an ancient river bed cross the road and the adjoining field at that point, it is quite different to the inclusionless silted deposits in the rest of the area.

It is assumed that the swift-flowing Monnow would eventually have cut through the neck of the loop to leave an oxbow-type of lagoon at Parc Glyndŵr (see reconstruction drawing by Peter Bere); the surface of the still water would have been quickly colonised by water pondweed while bullrushes and other lakeside plants would have thrived along its edges. The lagoon was then beginning to turn into a swamp so that eventually the pondweed died and gave way to the marsh and bog conditions which created a layer of peat across the site.

The alternative interpretation is that the river bed and bank revealed at Parc Glyndŵr was where the Monnow dropped the material it was carrying on entering the quieter waters of the lake but when the great lake drained, the river took up its present course, leaving an isolated smaller lagoon which then began its journey through the lake to bog phases. This explanation would perhaps fit well with the time allowed between the draining of the lake and its silting up.

The archaeological record at Parc Glyndŵr shows that the shores of the vast lake, where it was joined by the busy River Monnow, had attracted human settlement for many thousands of years – from the Stone Ages through the Bronze Age and into the Iron Age; in fact the only period when occupation was apparently sparse was during Roman times when the Monnow had taken its present course and little was left of the post-glacial lake or of its lagoon.

The lake had changed into boggy, curlew-haunted fields and is now experiencing a new age of settlement – just another phase in a long history.

Alluvial deposits left by the ancient River Monnow where it joined the post-glacial lake

The bed of the post-glacial lake covered by a thin layer of pondweed marl (white) and peat (black) after the forming of the 'lagoon following the draining of the lake

The pondweed marl beneath the peat over the bed of the lake and the 'lagoon'

The gravel of the lake bed spread across the whole area under excavation

The graded sands and gravels on the bank of the ancient River Monnow where it entered the post-glacial lake

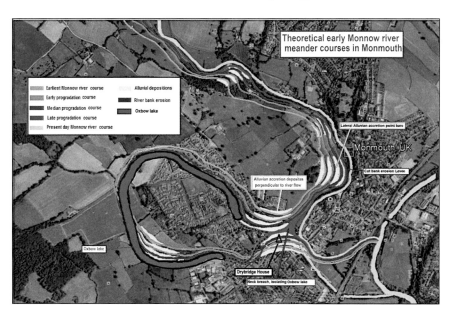

Peter Bere's reconstruction of the meandering River Monnow Parc Glyndŵr is the light-coloured field at the upper left of the loop

CHAPTER FIVE

A Rather Big Mystery

During the excavations for the attenuation pond we had recorded and removed two burnt mounds under the requirements of the council's archaeological advisers and were watching the digging of the latest mound when three fifteen metre long strips of light grey clay appeared. They were crossing a third burnt mound.

The lines were shallow channels filled with light-coloured clay and were pointing towards the west – the deepest part of the lagoon and presumably the lake; they later proved to be level and precisely parallel, over 27 metres long and fading towards the edge of the lake.

We found that the lines were shallow linear channels filled with anaerobic clay; the two larger ones had round bottoms – like the sides of trees while the smaller one was more 'chisel-shaped,'

PARC GLYNDŴR was proving to be a fascinating site – we had discovered two Bronze Age burnt mounds (later there proved to be seven) within an area less than thirty metres long, together with a New Stone Age hearth. The mounds were to have individual radio-carbon dates of from c1090BC up to c1815BC (*Appendix B*) and the Neolithic hearth one of around a thousand years earlier.

It was on a sunny Saturday afternoon while Hazel, my wife, and I were watching the digging of the last fifteen metres of the attenuation pond that the three light-coloured clay strips appeared; they were running westwards across a third burnt mound. The strips turned out to be 'channels' filled with anaerobic clay and were standing out starkly against the background of red clay and the dark, fire-cracked stones of the burnt mound. We found that the channels appeared to have been cut from the very surface of the burnt mound which was lying under the centre of the features.

We got the digger-driver to check all around and proved that the channels were continuing to the west but were otherwise isolated. So we set about cleaning and surveying them before trying to understand what they were. The developers agreed to suspend the work on that part of the site for some months.

Two of the channels proved to be shallow and round-bottomed 'cuts', with the narrower, eastern one, being of an inverted trapezoidal shape. The widest of the three was almost a metre across but only around 0.20m deep. The middle one was a little narrower but otherwise was very similar – with the same rounded bottom.

An odd aspect was that the bottoms of all three were on a similar level. From the edge of the new attenuation pond to the end of the excavated area was some 15 metres (around 50 feet) with the lines continuing into the section on the west. We were later to discover that they were nearly twice that length.

At first we thought that the channels were the foundations for a large building, perhaps a longhouse. There were huge longhouses known in the Neolithic but this was Bronze Age or later for it was post-dating one of the burnt mounds. The rounded shape of the channels, as well as their lengths, at first seemed to be the relics of sleeper beams made with whole trees and laid out perfectly parallel to each other. These were clearly quite extraordinary remains, especially as the cuts were so accurate – almost resembling work of a later age – and cut into the surface of the burnt mound with no sign of a build-up of soil before they were made. This suggested that they were of a similar age to the burnt mound. Furthermore, the overburden above the mound, which had built up since the channels were formed, was a metre thick. So it appeared pretty certain that the channels were not a lot later than the burnt mound – which was to produce a date of c1750BC (*Appendix*).

The other important characteristic of the stratification was that the site had not been ploughed down from a higher level. This was amply demonstrated by the total absence of any disturbance to the surface of the burnt mound – tilling of any kind would have mixed the stones with the anaerobic clay fill of the channels but both features were lying with clean, unbroken edges.

Sir Barry Cunliffe later kindly looked at the photographs and commented that they reminded him of 'lazy beds' which are linear mounded strips separated by shallow ditches. But of course, once again cultivation of this kind would have mixed the stones with the clay and planting across the burnt mound would not have taken place without disturbing or removing the burnt stones. Well over a hectare of ground (10,000 square metres) in the immediate area of the channels was excavated; proving conclusively that the channels were isolated and not part of some agricultural system. Far larger adjoining areas were stripped of peat or trenched during the construction of 85 houses or during landscaping around the attenuation pond but once again no comparable features were revealed. There was no sediment in any of the channels.

I judged that the mound and the cuts were not long separated in time and had probably been undisturbed since the site was abandoned – some time during the Bronze Age.

We were later to find that one of the significant aspects of the channels was that they were so close to the level of the water in the lake and although they may have been just clear of the water they appear to have been flooded (during the winter?) – hence the development of the anaerobic clay fill. This indicates that the channels, whatever their purpose, were closely associated with the lake and were probably the result of a seasonal activity.

An essential aspect of the channels was that all three contained a few flakes of flint – some very small but all with sharp clean breaks (there is no local flint). This convinces me that the slots were associated with wood working.

The channels looked as though they were 'fossils' left by rotted timbers – perhaps 'sleeper beams' or 'soleplates' of a building or buildings but they were comparatively huge. Two of the channels, in looking like the sides of trees, also looked like the bottoms of boats.

Several archaeologists came to see the site and I e-mailed pictures to other people but no-one had any suggestions as to what they might be.

Current Archaeology ran an article on 'Monmouth's Mystery Monuments' and quoted the wetland expert Francis Pryor who said that he had 'never seen anything like the Monmouth site' and that 'This shows we don't begin to understand the diversity and complexity of burnt mounds.' 'What an extraordinary site.'

I wrote to Francesco Menotti, Professor of Archaeology at the Institute of Prehistory and Archaeological Science, Basel University, Switzerland who is one of the leading wetland specialists in Europe, asking if he was interested. He replied with enthusiasm (7th June 2012) and has continued with help and advice throughout the excavation.

+ + +

A meeting was taking place while we were trowelling up the channels (as I was to call them later) and the managing director of Charles Church, Mr Steve Williams, said that he was happy for us to publish the discoveries. By this time I thought that it had to be some sort of structure, set on massive wooden foundations – a 'longhouse' perhaps – a name which was to come back to haunt me. Professor Menotti suggested that the slots might be to take some sort of frame-work.

Meanwhile, back on the site, Gordon McDonald and Jane Bray, now joined by Peter Bere, continued to develop their 'prehistoric boatyard' theories – Peter producing a lively reconstruction drawing of the launching of one of the Parc Glyndŵr craft (page 100).

During November we extended the excavation beyond the western end towards the lake and the deepest part of the 'lagoon' or lake. In appalling weather we found that the channels continued for a least 89 feet (27.12 metres) – while remaining perfectly parallel and level; in fact Dr Neil Phillips, while surveying the remains, was intrigued to find a difference of just 5mm between the previously excavated Channel 1 and its extension. The new trenches flooded as we dug them.

However, strange things were happening – as they neared the edge of the lake the channels were changing colour and fading into the surrounding clay.

Because the level of the bed of the lake and the surface of the burnt mound were so similar to each other, the anaerobic clay filling the channels may have formed through silting under water; this happened to the excavated channels during prolonged wet weather before the end of the excavation. The silting would have come with flooding with the rising and falling of the lake or, of course, the channels may have been purposely flooded. I see the anaerobic clay as further evidence that the channels were closely associated with the water level in the lake and were probably open shortly after the burnt mound was abandoned.

The three channels during exposure, looking north-west

The western section looking north-west

The three channels (channel 1 is on the right) looking west

The new attenuation pond and the three channels cut across the surface of Burnt Mound 3, looking east

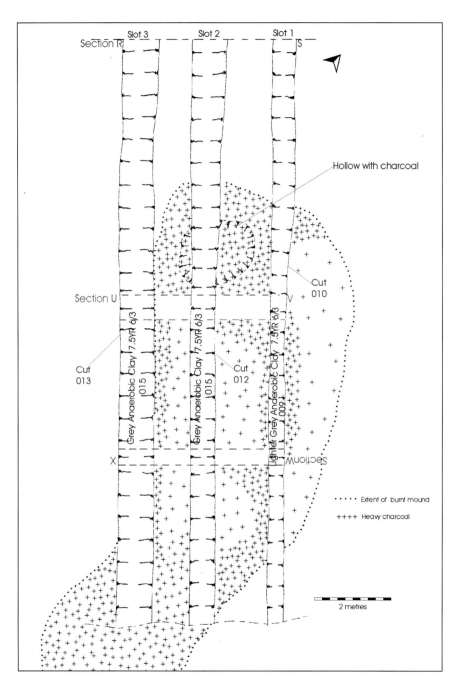

The eastern end of the channels cut across Burnt Mound 3. Some edges have crumbled but the channels were perfectly parallel to each other and very level

Channel 2 (top right) cut across the surface burnt mound 3, looking north

Channel 2, looking west and showing that it was the cut from close
the level of the surface level of the burnt mound

Channel 3. West is at the top

*Trapezoidal Channel 1, looking west and showing that the channels
were cut from close to the level of the surface level of the burnt mound*

Channel 1 running across Burnt Mound 3, looking west

Channel 1, cut into the surface of the burnt mound

CHAPTER SIX

Strange things
At the bottom of the Lake

During the stripping of the peat for the central roadway at Parc Glyndŵr, two perfectly parallel peat-filled 'hollows' were revealed; they were pointing towards the centre of the lagoon and were round-bottomed and very straight, although sloping over what we believed to be the edge of the lagoon.

We dreamed up all manner of explanations but none seemed feasible. However, in retrospect, the problem seems to have been that we were seeing the features as cuts filled with peat rather than the 'ghosts' of rotted 'things' then filled with peat.

Parts of the two 'things' seem to have been drawn up partially out of the lagoon.

An important aspect was that they were lying on top of a very thin layer of pondweed marl which had later accumulated on each side of the features before the production of the peat. The indication was that the hollows were created after the lake had drained and during the early days in the life of the lagoon.

DURING excavations for the foundations of the middle roadway at Parc Glyndŵr the peat was stripped down to the lime marl and it was then that two peat-filled hollows were revealed; they were running in very straight parallel lines – pointed towards the deepest part of the lagoon – as it appears today. The hollows were approximately 10 metres in length, with both ends continuing under the sections and in part reaching beyond the layer of pondweed marl (east) but not beyond the peat, which filled and covered the hollows; this is interpreted as their being partially out of the lake (and the lagoon).

The depths of the hollows, which had been truncated during the builder's excavations, ranged from over 0.20m on the east, to around 0.10m on the west. These depths depended upon the thickness of the lime marl for no sides could be distinguished in the peat.

An important aspect was that they were lying on top of an early (very thin) phase of pondweed marl which had then accumulated on each side before the production of the peat began. This appears to show that the 'hollows' were created at the end of the life of the post glacial lake.

The widths of the hollows varied according to how much they were truncated during the excavations but considering the reduced level they were from about 0.60m to around 0.95m wide.

Further to the east there was a pebbly band running across the excavation where the two hollows appeared to end but no close study of that area was achieved. The hollows here were sunk into the sandy layer below the pondweed marl on the east and into the marl on the west. It seems that the eastern ends of the features were originally outside the lake and partially sunk in the sandy bank.

The strange hollows inspired a number of bizarre explanations amongst the diggers (eg Roman vineyards) but the defining aspect was that they must have been in place during the early phase of the creation of the pondweed marl at the bottom of the lake and before being covered by peat during the swamp/marsh phase. If the peat had accumulated at the rate suggested in various studies around the world (some 0.5mm per year) we could have been looking towards some two thousand years in the deeper parts of the lagoon. Besides the peat, we wondered how long it would have taken to build up the various layers of clay covering the peat and equally the layer of pondweed marl beneath it.

At first we assumed that the features had been hollowed out or very cleanly cut into the lime marl underneath the peat. I drew plans and cut several sections before cleaning out a length of both hollows but that produced nothing – they simply appeared as very straight peat-filled hollows set into the marl.

In retrospect, of course, it seems that the problem was simply that I was thinking of the hollows as *cuts* – like shallow *trenches* – which I was to find later, was wrong.

It was during the excavation for the attenuation pond that I realised that the strange round-bottomed cuts there, this time on dry land overlooking the ancient lake, were similar to the things at the bottom of the lagoon although they were not level and the one was filled with clay and the other with peat.

The area of the lagoon is shown on one of John Sorrell's air photographs and extends to around halfway across the site. The pondweed marl must mark the water line but the peat continues outside the spread of marl. The hollows appeared to widen towards the east (the eastern side of the lake) but this was probably caused by the variation in the depth of truncation during the peat stripping.

Around 12cms of pondweed lime marl had accumulated each side of the hollows retaining their original rounded shape and this contrasted strongly with the peat filling and covering the hollow.

It appears that two long and very straight objects, probably made of wood and resembling two wide telegraph poles, were sunk, side by side, in the lake when the production of the pondweed marl began near the shore of the lake.

The sequence appears to be that the objects were in place in still water during the early days of the silting of the lagoon and survived long enough to retain its rounded shape after the lake became a swamp or marsh and the peat phase began; presumably the peat then filled the void left by the totally rotted objects.

On the other hand, if the objects were originally hollow like dugouts, the peat must have filled them after the pondweed had died out – this would have to mean that, if dugouts, the sides were high enough to prevent the marl from entering the inside (with roots in the lake bed).

The time taken for the marl to accumulate and wood to rot is paramount in deciding if the features were hollow or solid although the pondweed would presumably have required its roots to be on the bed of the lake.

+   +   +

Another anomaly in the bed of the lake was discovered as this book was at the proof stage – in August 2013 – because of its association with vast numbers of snails has been slipped into Chapter 10 : The Environment.

Rotting of timbers

During discussions with archaeologists who had not visited the site it was explained to me that the channels cutting across Burnt Mound 3 had never contained timbers because they would have taken too long to decay. However, although they were right about there never having been timbers permanently in the channels, they were wrong about the speed of wood decay. This is not the type of wetland as are the Fens, where timbers can be preserved for thousands of years, but wet and dry land which causes rapid decay of organic material. Only under exceptional circumstances is wood preserved – even on medieval sites – in Monmouth. Even bones by Roman times are normally so soft that they can be sliced through with a trowel by accident. The Iron Age bones from the bed of the lake are an unusual exception for them, and a few pieces of timber, were sealed from the peat by the pondweed marl which may explain the anomaly for nothing at all was found preserved in the peat.

The evidence is the same from sites such as Flag Fen where rapid decay takes hold once the wetland dries out; the winter 2012-13 edition of *Rescue News* ran an article describing the desiccation of Flag Fen where it was claimed that the timbers will have gone in fifty years if the money for preservation is not found.

Evidence from Parc Glyndŵr is common. For instance, a substantial timber which was pre-dated by a field drain laid by Cyril Ward in the 1950s was found lying over the layer of peat on the site. The wood had become so soft that a trowel sank through it with hardly any pressure and during the attempted lifting the whole piece crumbled into small fragments; the largest fragment was 6cm long. If this has taken just half a century it seems that little would be left from the Bronze or Iron Ages.

A possible interpretation, by Peter Bere

The parallel linear peat-filled features in the lagoon, looking north

The parallel truncated features (0.60m and 0.950m wide), looking west

The peat-filled hollow is bounded by the pondweed marl, retaining the rounded shape of the object. The thin layer of marl, running under the hollow, shows that the feature is the ghost of something sunk and rotted in the lake after the lake became a lagoon. This feature was close to the edge of the lagoon and at an early stage of silting

A section showing that the round-bottomed object lay over a thin layer of sand (where there was is no pondweed marl). This seems to have been partly outside the edge of the lagoon and was later filled with and covered by peat.

A section showing that the round-bottomed object (which was truncated during the stripping of the peat) was lying on top of a very thin band of the pondweed marl.

This apparently means that the object was sunk in the lagoon soon after the pondweed marl had began to form and before it had accumulated on each side of the object. This must have been shortly after the draining of the main post-glacial lake and the forming of the lagoon.

Peat later filled the hollow and covered the area as the lagoon went through its swamp to marsh to bog phases.

An unexplained feature, possibly a rotted post, in the bed of the lake, filled with the pondweed marl and just to the left of the northern hollow

The 'ghost' of one of the objects (top left to bottom right) after the removal of the peat. The feature is lying on a thin layer of pondweed marl (white) which must have been laid down after the draining of the lake when the lagoon was in the early stages of silting

A fifty-year-old timber lying across the field drain (right-hand side)

The timber lying across a drain laid in the 1950s; it is in an advanced stage of decomposition

A tree bowl in the 'lagoon', filled with peat and with just a few fragments of preserved root remaining

CHAPTER SEVEN

What have we discovered?

There was considerable prehistoric activity around the post-glacial lake from at least the Middle Stone Age and it continued through the New Stone Age, the Bronze Age and into the Iron Age.

It was obvious that whatever they were, the prehistoric features overlooking the lake at Parc Glyndŵr were linked to activities on the lake.

THAT the post-glacial lake which once filled the Monmouth basin and had survived into the late Iron Age appears to have been established through stratified remains and radiocarbon dates associated with alluvial deposits at around the 21m OS level in the higher parts of Monmouth town.

Considering the area and levels of the alluvium and the gravel terraces around Monmouth it follows that the lake must have extended to the edges of the Parc Glyndŵr development site. On the site, the bed of the lake bed was consistently around 23m OD which means that the alluvial deposits around upper Monmouth arrived from at least 2m of water.

There is convincing evidence that the River Monnow joined the lake on the Parc Glyndŵr site and that a lagoon was formed when the Ice Age blockage of the Wye Valley, to the south of Monmouth, was breached to drain the area. The draining appears most likely to have taken place during the later Iron Age.

+   +   +

Human Activity beside the lake

The evidence for prehistoric activity on the gravel terraces overlooking the lake at Parc Glyndŵr begins in the New Stone Age with a radiocarbon date from charcoal inside a stone-surrounded hearth of c2795BC (*Appendix B*). The hearth contained fragments of cremated bone and a small flint. Other flints from beside the lake include a Bronze Age scraper fashioned from a fragment of a New Stone Age polished axe and a small flint blade which might be of Middle Stone Age date – the same period as the hunter-gatherer campsite on the shore of the lake in St James' Street.

The Bronze Age is particularly well represented with at least seven burnt mounds, four of them with radiocarbon dates ranging from c1090BC to c1815BC. There is also an assemblage of Bronze Age pottery from one of the burnt mounds with a date of c1750BC (*Appendix B*).

Iron Age settlement, temporary or otherwise, is confirmed by an assemblage of animal bone (domestic waste) from the bottom of the lake/lagoon (south) which has produced a radiocarbon date of c525BC. The iron slag recovered from a post- or late-lagoon stream bed towards the end of the watching brief may be Iron Age but seems more likely to be Roman. An area of charcoal on the clay over the peat near the northern edge of the lake/lagoon produced a date of c490BC and the Bronze Age flint scraper.

By Roman times the lake on the development site had been replaced by the lagoon and was becoming a swamp or a marsh from where a peat sample produced a radiocarbon date of cAD195. A sherd of Samian Ware from the anaerobic clay above the peat is dated to AD240-300 (Dr Peter Webster). The only other Roman pottery find was an unstratified sherd of

Black Burnished ware from the bottom of the modern western drainage ditch. The iron slag recovered Roman.

These dates indicate that the lake still existed during the Iron Age but it and the lagoon were silted up by Roman times; this is supported by the late Iron Age pottery and radiocarbon date of 100BC from St James' Street.

+   +   +

In relation to the Lake

The lake must have been the attraction for this extended human activity and it seems inevitable that there would have been lacustrine undertakings on the water itself while the suggested tidal access to the sea is reason to be aware of the maritime possibilities.

+   +   +

The channels cut across Burnt Mound 3

The three channels were consistently parallel, at least 90 feet long (27m), they were very level, quite straight and aligned with the deepest part of the peat in the lake or lagoon (roughly north-west to south-east). The two wider channels (Channels 2 and 3) are round-bottomed while Channel 1 is narrower and trapezoidal; this channel also has a fill of lighter coloured anaerobic clay than the other two.

That the channels were close to the level of the lake surface must be significant, as must be the fact that they are cut from the very surface of the burnt mound – the stratification suggesting that they may not be a lot later than the abandonment of the mound. This is supported by the absence of any datable material from the channels other than sharp flakes of imported flint which were found in all three channels. A radiocarbon date of c1750BC, gained from charcoal in one of the channels – well away from the burnt mound – is of interest but it does not support a later date for the feature but of course it does not prove or disprove that the channels are a lot later than the burnt mound either. That is indicated by the metre of undisturbed overburden sealing the mound and the channels.

+   +   +

The suggestion made by archaeologists who have not been to the site, that the channels were dug for 'water management' (drains?), is manifestly untenable: the channels are remarkably level, very straight and perfectly parallel to one another; there are no V or U shapes – just consistently rounded or trapezoidal-shaped bottoms and with no sediments. The three channels, of two different types, are isolated and, although heading for the lake, otherwise seem to be going nowhere; also, if they were meant to hold level water for any length of time, it would have been lost as the channels cut across the burnt mound.

The total absence of disturbance between the channels and the burnt mound is surely the ultimate evidence ruling out drains or ploughing as well as 'lazy beds'; the latter – linear mounds between ditches – normally cover large areas and research shows that they follow the lie of the land and are never very level or perfectly parallel to each other.

The idea that the channels were soleplates for a structure (the wider two being like complete trees), which I had originally thought, had to be quickly abandoned – unfortunately after it had been in the press (I should have known better). Since then Dr Martin Bates of Trinity Saint David University could find no trace of timber in the clay fill. However, it is most likely that the sharp fragments of flint were flakes from tools used in wood working and this is important evidence for the use of the channels and at an early period.

The profile of the two larger channels matches the size and shape of trees but if the channels had been the setting for large timbers they must have been entirely removed. Considering the evident relationship of the channels to the lake it is almost certain that the completed timbers were slid out onto the lake – explaining the purpose of the channels.

If the channels were created for the working of timbers and for moving the finished result to the lake they may have been roughly dug before the timbers were put in place and extended on completion of the work. The channels cut into the very plastic clay overlooking the lake would of course have to match the shape of the finished product. The channels would then be lubricated with water or even flooded and the object moved along to the lake – the hardest part being getting the thing started as it may have sunk into the ground (deepening the shape of the matrix). Once it was moving (with more water being thrown around) the product should slip easily along to the lake. I have seen a 14 ton machine, with tracks, sliding on the wet clay of the adjoining building site, so with enough hands, the new wooden frame should be no problem. For this, the channels would need to be level, parallel and straight, which they are. They may not have been primarily for keeping the timbers stable while working as their weight would probably have done that. Compared with making the dugouts or more complex combinations, the digging of the channels would be no problem and could probably be done by a small team in a few hours.

That the three channels were linked is evident from the fact that they are perfectly parallel, level and straight. If the three imagined 'timbers' were moved towards the lake they would have been moved together, as a frame.

+   +   +

The peat-filled features – beached on the shore of the lake?

It may be that the round-bottomed 'hollows' in the lagoon are the 'ghosts' of totally rotted wooden objects. The two hollows have the appearance of having been scooped out in precisely parallel, straight sloping lines,

80

through the peat and into the pondweed marl. As the peat filling the hollows was the same as that covering them and as rhat on each side of their upper parts – no cuts were discernible. It seems unlikely that there ever had been a cut but that the two 'hollows' were the result of solid objects having rotted after being abandoned as the lake was changing to a lagoon during the Iron Age.

The hollows were aligned with what appears to be the deepest part of the lagoon (roughly east-west). Except that there are two of them, they otherwise appear to have been isolated, as the features on the burnt mound. The pondweed marl stops at the sides of the hollows, having accumulated against things with curved sides.

If the marl had built up each side of a log or boat, the resulting hollow would not have received any pondweed lime marl until the log had rotted away which may have been after the production of marl had been succeeded by that of peat. This might be seen as suggesting that they are the 'ghosts' of logs; however, the pondweed would presumably have its roots in the bed of the lake so that no marl would have collected inside a canoe until it had completely rotted away. The length of time that a log or canoe would take to rot and how quickly the pondweed marl would have accumulated are things we do not know.

The possible range of decomposed objects is probably limited to a choice between two large round solid timbers or two long hollow canoes. Such imagined objects may, as they were parallel to each other, have been joined together and been partially beached onto the shore of the lake or lagoon. The possibility that these are traces of a raft (long round timbers), individual or twinned canoes, or even a more complex combination seems reasonable to me.

In the Lake

The twin features in the lake or lagoon bear a strong resemblance to the two larger channels on the burnt mound – being straight and precisely parallel (but not level). There is, however, a problem. The 'matrix' on the mound should be Bronze Age while the 'ghost' in the lake appears to sit on an Iron Age lake bed.

+   +   +

Sizes. The features in the lake are at least ten metres long which seems at first sight to be excessive for dugout hulls or canoes. However, the preserved Bronze Age canoes discovered at Must Farm, Cambridgeshire, were up to 8m long, while one at Hanson Quarry, Shardlo, Derbyshire, was 10m long; the Lurgan Boat was even longer, so it appears that the length does not affect the possibilities that the Parc Glyndŵr remains are shades of maritime craft. Presumably if we are dealing with log rafts rather than log boats they could easily be longer again although solid logs would surely be less manageable.

CHAPTER EIGHT

The Case for Prehistoric Boats at Parc Glyndŵr

In 1998, the Channel 4 Time Team carried out trial excavations at Smallhythe in Kent to explore the site of a major medieval shipyard on the banks of the River Rother. Large ships were built and launched from the site so the excavations were expected to reveal dry docks and inlets into the estuary. Surprisingly, the site contained nothing of the sort. However, what was discovered has extraordinary similarities to the Bronze Age remains at Parc Glyndŵr – although the two are separated by thousands of years.

IN THE Introduction I compared the prehistoric remains at Parc Glyndŵr with those at the medieval shipyard at Smallhythe in Kent. I suggested that the technologies of many ancient industries had not changed over centuries, sometimes millennia, and that, although separated by thousands of years, the two sites had a great deal in common. Could this be a coincidence or is it parallel modus operandi?

Excavations by Channel 4s Time Team had shown at Smallhythe that the prevailing ideas of how medieval boats were constructed and launched had been quite wrong. There were none of the expected inlets to the estuary or enclosed docks, for vessels were constructed in channels dug into the ground and shaped like the bottoms of the boats being built.

Although smaller, the Monmouth channels were also aligned on the shore of the lake at right angles to the water and with very level bases. The wood working evidence at Smallhythe came from ships' nails in the channels while at Monmouth it came from sharp flakes of flint in the channels.

The one channel which was excavated had been cut into the bank of the estuary just above high tide level and at right angles to the water; it had a level base upon which a keel would have been laid. These aspects were comparable with the Monmouth boat-shaped channels which were also set very close to the water level.

The possibility that the channels were meant to be flooded from the lake in order to float craft straight out onto the surface of the lake appears very likely; and the shallower water at Parc Glyndŵr would have made that shore preferable for constructing and launching boats rather than the steeply shelving banks and deep water of the lake around Monmouth.

The requirements for travelling on rivers, lakes and oceans did not change – requiring craft which had to be constructed on land and launched from land – so I suggest that we might reasonably assume that similar systems to those revealed during excavations at Smallhythe could have been used during prehistoric times. This would be consistent with practices in many other industries during periods prior to the Industrial Revolution.

Parc Glyndŵr lies along the edge of a silted up lake while Smallhythe is on the edge of a silted up estuary and today both are some ten miles from the sea. Like Smallhythe, the Monmouth site appears to have had safe access to the sea while both sites had extensive raw materials in the form of dense woodland.

During the Middle Ages Smallhythe was one of the largest shipyards in the country when the River Rother provided access to the sea for huge vessels such as some of the largest warships used in the Hundred Years War. These included the ships which carried Henry V's troops to France for the Battle of Agincourt in 1415.

We now believe that the three channels may be the template for the construction of a prehistoric boat or boats and that some of the remains in the lagoon may also be the 'shade' of a vessel or of vessels.

The situation of the remains across burnt mound 3, overlooking a post-glacial lake, which survived into the Iron Age and with access to the sea, is clearly important, as is the number and types of prehistoric sites along the shore of the lake. If the lake existed – and we know that it did; if the occupations existed – and we have proved they did – then it is certain there would have been people messing about in boats.

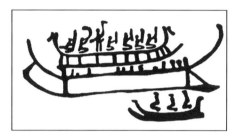

Scandinavian Rock Art Outrigger and crew

Ethnographic and now archaeological evidence from Europe and around the world supports the speculations of several eminent British archaeologists that craft with stabilisers or outriggers did exist and were in action along the Atlantic Seaboard during prehistoric times and especially during the Bronze Age. Indeed, engravings of boats with unmistakable outriggers are depicted in Scandinavian Bronze Age rock art.

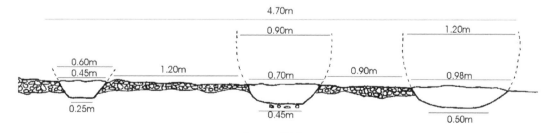

Section W-X

The two larger round-bottomed channels at Parc Glyndŵr are shaped like the sides of trees but of course they are also shaped like the bottoms of boats, as was the channel at Smallhythe, and we suggest that they were where large timbers were set shallowly in the ground, creating a stable base to work with flint, metal axes and possibly fire. If twin dugouts were the product, their precisely parallel positions suggest that they were joined together – with or without a light superstructure and a sail. The third (trapezoidal) channel, which was level and parallel with the other two channels, appears most likely to have been a related, possibly integral, part of the combination – an outrigger. Such a finished combination could have been slid along the watered or purposely flooded parallel and level channels before being launched into the lake which in this area was very close to the level of the land.

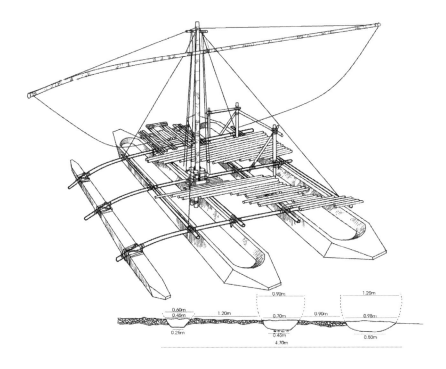

Peter Bere's reconstruction of a Parc Glyndŵr Boat
Based on the archaeological features

Such contrivances, unwieldy in construction, might be very sturdy and probably capable of making extended crossings of deep water. Williams records that the Fijians' double canoes, which are similar to the craft envisaged at Monmouth, were capable of carrying a hundred people and tons of goods. They could cover a thousand miles of ocean (Williams, T. Fiji and the Fijians, Vol II, 1858, London, A Heylin)

Double canoes would also be worthy vessels on large lakes, for Graham Symonds, of Monmouth Canoe Hire, told me that the swell on a lake of this size could be considerable and that he had personal experience of rowing on Llandegfedd Reservoir, when the oars acted as stabilisers. Perhaps single dugouts were mainly used around the shores of large lakes and on the rivers.

One of the vessels recorded in Fiji sounds very similar to our vision of the Parc Glyndŵr twin-hulled outriggers:

"The drua, or double canoe, differs from the rest in having another smaller canoe for its outrigger and the deck is laid across both."

These craft had to be constructed on dry land but very close to water and to the level of its surface. Other requirements would include the sort of countryside in which large trees can root and thrive; this would tend to rule out areas such as the Cotswolds or the mountainous zones.

There could also be problems in launching large vessels along some coasts, for instance the Severn Estuary with its deep and extensive estuarine mud does not strike me as being ideal. The twin hulls with outriggers envisaged at Parc Glyndŵr would have been almost five metres wide and, if they were similar to the Lurgan boat, some 15 metres long.

Parc Glyndŵr meets all the requirements, including having 'plastic' clay for the almost water level channels. The length of such vessels would not be so important for I imagine that keeping the flat bottom of the craft level would be easier within the channels. In fact, I find it hard to suggest any other interpretation for the remains – from the setting, to the dating – Parc Glyndŵr appears to fit the picture.

I have also suggested that the chances of discovering a preserved prehistoric vessel of the kind envisaged at Monmouth is far lower than it would be of finding the more unstable solo logboats. Paired boats or boats with outriggers seem more likely to have completed their lives on water intact and have been broken up on land rather than being lost on the water to be preserved under anaerobic conditions.

However, it appears that a part of one has been found – at Lurgan in Ireland – one which may match the Monmouth matrix. There is part of another similar boat at Carrowneden, also in Ireland. The Lurgan logboat has features which indicate that it had been fitted to another boat or an outrigger.

The arrival at the National Museum of Ireland of the huge log boat from Addergoole Bog, Lurgan, County Galway, in 1902.
The boat has features suggesting that it had an outrigger or was joined to another log boat.

Both of the Irish boats are of a similar period to the Monmouth burnt mound cut by the channels: The Lurgan boat radiocarbon date was 3940 ± 25 BP and the Carrowneden one 3890 ± 80 BP. The radiocarbon dates obtained from the Bronze Age Burnt Mound 3 – the one cut by the Parc Glyndŵr channels – is 3700 ± 35 BP and it is noted that Channel 3 is the same width as that of the Lurgan boat.

+   +   +

In the 19th century ocean-going boats were again built in Monmouth and launched into the River Wye – but this time they were up to 400 tons in weight.

One of the last of the maritime boats to be built here, appropriately named *The Monmouth*, turned over during sideways launching near the Wye Bridge in 1825 and two people were drowned. However, it is evident that if Bronze Age boats had gained tidal access over the Ice Age blockage of the Wye Valley, or been beached and re-floated below it, they could easily have reached the sea.

+   +   +

During the final excavations for the attenuation pond an area of charcoal was revealed five metres to the south of Burnt Mound No 3 and an unusually large piece of charcoal was recovered (at SO 49290 13103). Although mostly less than 5mm thick the charcoal appears to represent a substantial plank-like fragment with a straight edge.

A sample of the charcoal was sent to the SUERC (Scottish Universities Environmental Research Centre) and produced a Bronze Age radiocarbon date consistent with the range of activities recorded earlier along the edge of the lake: 1248-1245 cal BC, 2899 ± 31 *SUERC-40260 (GU30722)*.

This is the youngest of the Bronze Age dates from the site and is further evidence of long-term activities beside the lake.

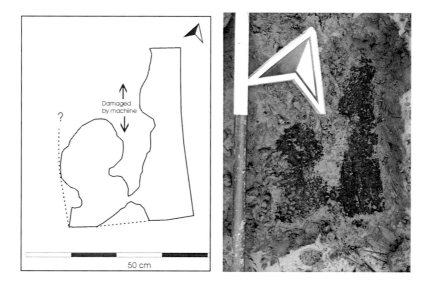

A Bronze Age timber turned to charcoal – near Burnt Mound 3

An Outrigger

Gordon McDonald e-mailed his thoughts that the likelihood is that the hulls of the Parc Glyndŵr boat were dugout oak. He wrote:

> As this could well be the case you can appreciate they would individually, never mind collectively, be very heavy. A complete boat in regular use would be hauled in and out of the water possibly every trip. Because the hulls are bare wood if they were left in the water the wood (even oak) would quickly become waterlogged. Skin covered 30ft Curraghs can be carried with ease by a small group of men, as I saw in 2000. However, in view of the size of a Parc Glyndŵr boat made of oak there is no way it could be carried. The act of dragging the hulls in and out of the lake regularly would in itself be sufficient to erode the channels into the Burnt Mound.

Gordon began his calculations:

> I have run some calculations on the estimated weight of the Parc Glyndŵr boat.
>
> Working on a dugout hull 45ft long with a 4ft beam and a hull thickness of no less than 2 inches (excluding any fittings or bow or stern extensions) and assuming it is built from native British Oak; I calculate the total dry timber weight to be just over 1.5 tons. I have also recalculated the figures in metric with an increased hull thickness and this comes out at over two metric tons per hull.
>
> It is very probable that the all-in weight of both dugout hulls and the outrigger together could well be over 3 (English) tons. You can see that carrying the Parc Glyndŵr boat out of the water would not be an option but dragging the craft ashore would quickly create eroded channels up which the hulls would slide, particularly if the level of the lake for most of the time was stable slightly lower than the bottom of these channels, the idea that launching would be eased with water poured by hand into the channels seems practical sense.
>
> We cannot be certain how long the Park Glyndŵr boat was, if it was shorter it would be lighter of course and I have based my calculations on oak for the hulls because that seems to be the most common material used for the dugouts. However, what seems to be clear is that the channels fitted one particular craft. If a variety of craft were using the same channels on the Burnt Mound any, even slight deviation, in the distance between the hulls would have flattened out the more or less precise edges of the channels.

CHAPTER NINE

Bronze Age Outriggers?

This chapter is a collection of notes and associated photographs which I feel is relevant to our study of prehistoric activity on and around the Monmouth Lake. It consists mostly of evidence that twin-hulled craft and boats with outriggers were in use in the distant past – for instance, there are rock art records of such vessels during the Bronze Age – the period suggested for their presence at Parc Glyndŵr. Ethnographic examples are also featured and there is a note on the Lurgan Boat together with quotes predicting prehistoric outriggers by some eminent archaeologists.

WE have seen that the Monmouth basin contained a huge post-glacial lake which survived until the late Iron Age and which attracted settlement from at least the time of the hunter-gatherers. In Monmouth town itself, a Middle Stone Age camp site and Iron Age occupation has been found on the shore of the lake, while a mile away, to the west, the lake was overlooked by another series of ancient settlements – settlements which constitute the main features of this book. There must be many other sites around the lake which lie under the deep overburden of silt turned to clay (often grey-green anaerobic clay) which we have shown covers much of the lake and the lagoon.

As mentioned, it would be remarkable indeed, considering the prehistoric settlements around this vast body of water, if there had been no lacustrine activity out on the lake itself.

I believe that we have shown that people were, indeed, exploiting the resources of the lake in boats and may even have gained access to the sea from the lake which must have been one of the most convenient places in the country in which to build and launch boats.

It seems likely that boats with outriggers would have enjoyed a higher survival rate than single dugouts and would therefore be more likely to have been broken up or re-cycled towards the end of their useful working lives; canoes, on the other hand, would be more often lost while out on the water and then preserved under anaerobic conditions to produce the preservation bias we find today. The paucity of preserved wood at Parc Glyndŵr is manifest.

It is clear that double canoes or boats with stabilisers would have been very useful far out on the lake as well as being vital in the estuaries or on the sea, whereas single hulls may have been more restricted to the rivers and around the edges of the lakes.

We are lucky to have ample evidence from Scandinavian rock art that boats with outriggers were being used during the Bronze Age. A re-assessment of the Irish Lurgan boat is of particular interest for, as the authors (M.E. Robinson, D.W. Shimwel and G. Cribbin) say, it has a greater potential than previously realised. Discovered during drainage operations on a raised bog at Townland, Co. Galway, in 1902 the vessel is over 15m long and more than a metre wide. In 1996 part of a similar vessel, also in oak, was found at Carrowneden, less than 20km to the north.

The really significant aspect from our point of view is the evidence that the Lurgan boat had attachments for a second boat or a stabiliser or an outrigger of some kind. In the Lurgan boat they have identified three separate series of holes; the first series of holes may be the most significant. Three pairings are located approximately 0.27m below the sheerline as this is to be seen in the most intact portion of the boat on the forward port side. The holes are 3.5m apart. The first pair is 3.0m from the stern and the last pair is 5.0m from the bow. The second series of holes is located c0.15m below the present-day sheerline; but not all of them survive but there were probably five pairs of c0.9m.

The final series of holes are in the floor of the vessel and are thought to be thickness gauges employed during hollowing the craft. The authors say that the key to understanding the craft may lie in the series of paired holes that it displays and in particular the three pairs located 'in the upturn of the floor'. The only feasible explanation for these holes is that they were incorporated as fixing points for the attachment either of another logboat or of stabilizers or an outrigger of some kind.

With the addition of stabilisers it is 'also possible that these logboats were used, not as river-or-lake craft but as sea-going vessels, confined mainly to coastal waters but venturing short open-sea crossings in favourable weather, they may have originated anywhere within the Irish realm'.

+   +   +

Although ethnographic evidence mostly concerns single canoes or boats with outriggers, double hulls with outriggers are also recorded; indeed one of the Scandinavian Bronze Age engravings may be of one (page 109) while others are known – such as the Fijian double canoe with outrigger (page 110).

If one of these craft was left in the lagoon, all that might now be traceable would be the truncated bottom of the two hulls and the outrigger in the pondweed marl – that is if the conditions had been right and a layer of the marl had been formed around them. Certainly the wood will have been long since gone.

It is tempting to see Channel 1 as the matrix for an outrigger. The cut is the same shape as many stabilisers on ethnographic examples and although also perfectly parallel to the other channels is set farther out, as it probably would have been.

Although there are not the conditions for the preservation of timber or other perishable materials I feel that we have recognised remains which are directly linked to lacustrine or even maritime undertakings associated with the Monmouth post-glacial lake.

+   +   +

Two quotations:
> In discussing the inherent instability of prehistoric log boats, Sir Barry Cunliffe, in his book *Facing the Ocean - The Atlantic and its Peoples* (2001) suggested that if stabilising timbers or even outriggers

had been attached at the waterline a vessel capable of sailing in more open water could be achieved. He noted that there was a rich ethnographic record that this was done elsewhere in the world. That "No such evidence has yet been found along the Atlantic seaboard, may be little more than an accident of survival."

Robert Van de Noort (Chris Catling, *Current Archaeology* 'Connected by the sea' 26-33, 275, Feb. 2013): '[There are] many gaps in the story of the evolution of boats and the ample proxy evidence for boats at an early date from food pits containing bones from seabirds, fish and sea mammals that must have been caught at sea; from fish hooks and harpoons, etc shows a diet rich in marine species. We also lack the evidence for other types of craft: rafts, for example, or composite log boats with outriggers . . .'

+   +   +

The discoveries at Parc Glyndŵr have shown the value of the area to science and history. Hopefully, steps can be taken to protect the sites around the shores of this ancient lake and especially those areas already lined up for development and adjoining Parc Glyndŵr.

Linear boat-shaped channel at Smallhythe in Kent – a medieval boat-building site with similar features to those of the Bronze Age at Parc Glyndŵr
Courtesy of Time Team. Neil Emmanuel ©Videotext Communications

Parc Glyndŵr linear boat-shaped Channel 3

Parc Glyndŵr linear boat-shaped Channel 3

Scandinavian Bronze Age rock art depicting boats and canoes with outriggers

Two sides of a Fijian double canoe with outrigger

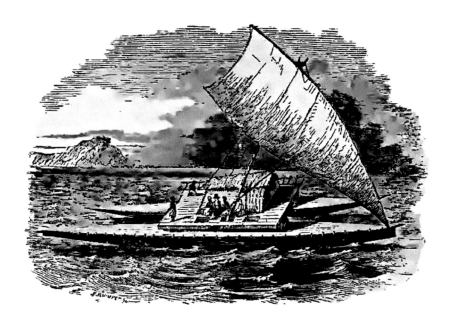

Channel 1 − The matrix shaped like an outrigger, during excavation

The three channels, looking from the east across the new attenuation pond, with the possible interpretation of twin hulls with an outrigger

Reconstruction de

Peter Bere's interpretation of the channels in use.

The features are not to scale and the attachments between the dugouts and the outrigger may have required sturdier timbers but the general idea is as the archaeologists on the site imagine a launching may have been.

Peter's drawing can be compared with the pictures of the Fijian double canoe and outrigger in action

CHAPTER TEN

Environmental

The soils of Parc Glyndŵr, although often associated with wet conditions, are not conducive to the preservation of organic material, at least with a few exceptions. The lagoon peat was notably low in preserved plant remains save for the occasional traces of decomposing wood on the bed of the lagoon and a tree bowl containing the partial remains of roots – the rest of the fill of that feature was indistinguishable from the peat itself.

Plant Life

THERE were impressive areas of marl beneath the peat of the lagoon – I have usually referred to it as 'lime marl'. The lime is taken from the water and deposited by *Potamogeton* pond weed and appears to mark an early phase in the life of the lagoon – where the lime was accumulating before the swamp/marsh phase and the peat dominated. It is white and can be in a very thin layer or at times over 0.15m thick; the quantity must presumably be directly related to the depth of the water. The lime produces a strong reaction to dilute hydrochloric acid and was generally devoid of organic remains except for the small assemblage of bones beneath it in the south-west corner of the lagoon and the huge numbers of molluscs in a few areas which were close to the edges of the lagoon.

The Animal Bones

by
ROSE DAVIS
Trinity Saint David University, Lampeter

The bone assemblage was recovered from the southern corner of the lake bed, below the lime marl and the peat. An Iron Age radiocarbon date was obtained from one of the bones: 766-484 cal BC, 2475 ± 35 BP, SUERC-41290 (GU27748), August 2012.

Methodology

The bones were identified using reference collections from Trinity Saint David University, Lampeter, with further guidance from Cohen & Searjeantson (1996), Hillson (1992) and Schmid (1972). Due to the absence of the diagnostic epiphyses of cattle and horse the large tibia and radius were assigned to the horse/cow category. The bones were also examined microscopically.

Bone and Species Representation

None of the bones are complete – consisting of long bone mid shafts, ie femur, metacarpal, metatarsal, humerus and radius representing cow, cow/horse, and sheep species. There is also a sheep canine tooth and two unidentifiable small pieces of bone.

Condition of Bones

Colour

All the bones are dark in colour, implying deposition in water, but there is no sign of the black staining on the bone surfaces due to manganese dioxide – a condition that is present when deposition in water has been permanent (Andrews 1995). Exposure to acid soil of between 3.5-4.5 ph results in shallow channels and circular pits (Nicholson 1996), but there is no sign of this.

Weathering

According to Behrensmeyer (1978) weathering has reached Stage 1 ie cracking, usually parallel to the orientation of the collagen fibres. Andrews (1995) concludes that some bones may have taken 10-12 years to reach Stage 1 (Behrensmeyer's study was on bones in the tropical savannah), and these bones may have taken a similar time to reach this weathering stage and therefore may have been exposed for some years before submergence in water.

Breakages

All the breakages on the bones can be classed as spiral, longitudinal and smooth perpendicular, with in all cases the loss of or rounding of what remains of the articular ends. As longitudinal and smooth perpendicular occurs when the bone is dry and weathered this again indicates the bone was exposed for some time before deposition. Spiral occurs when the bone is fresh and green (Marshall 1989), caused by twisting of the bone to extract the marrow. Some parts of the skeleton have a far better chance of survival than others. Bones that fuse late have thin walls and a spongy texture, unlike early fusing bones which are generally dense and compact and more resistant to decay, fragmentation and carnivore attack (Grant 1975). The late fusing bones are the proximal humerii and tibiae, proximal and distal end of the femora and distal end of the radii and these are all absent from this collection.

Bone breakages are due to many different causes:-

1.Trampling

Trampling, represented by striation marks, indicates pressure on the bones within deposits and all the bones examined show striation marks. Stone tools can mimic striation marks but some proportion of sedimentary particles can possess sharp edges that will, when enough force is exerted, cause a striation mark that is morphologically similar to stone tool marks, therefore it is practically impossible to allow absolute diagnosis between causal agents (Fisher 1995). The cow humerus shows signs of spiral and longitudinal breakage, indicating it was broken when fresh and then broken again at a later stage

2. Butchery

Although the cow/horse tibia and cow metacarpal display longitudinal cuts these are not the sharp edges caused by knives, but are probably due to trampling of the dry weathered bones, or breakage by carnivores. Under the microscope none of the bones display the characteristic v shaped marks caused by metal knives.

3. Carnivores

It used to be thought that spiral breakages to extract marrow were due exclusively to human activity, but Binford (1981) has shown that the practice is not unique to humans, but has also been observed in carnivores. Under a microscope the horizontal marks on the cow tibia, humerus and radius are U-shaped and probably caused by carnivore chewing. There are no marks on the metapodial shafts indicative of their low meat content. The distal end of the humerus and metatarsal reveal signs of abrasion and rounding, which could be attributed to the gnawing of the ends by carnivores, and the absence on all the bones of the proximal ends indicates the complete consumption of the meatier end (Lyman 1994).

4. Cooking

There is no evidence for burning. None of the bones show calcination or discolouration due to exposure to fire and stewed bone would have been paler and more degraded.

Some of the Iron Age bones from the bed of the
post-glacial lake
Photograph by John Bray

Conclusion
5. Fluvial Action
Fluvial action can result in abrasion due to the application of current driven, sediment laden water on bone surfaces, causing the rounding of articular ends. Also corrosion in wet and sheltered conditions can resemble carnivore gnawed articular ends.

The evidence presented on the bones in this collection indicates that they were probably exposed for some time to weathering processes during which they were broken due to trampling and carnivore predation. Some may have been broken for a second time at a later date. There is no evidence for exposure to acid on the bones from the peat formation occurring above. There is also no evidence of butchery or cooking on these bones – although roasted bone is brittle and more easily destroyed and some may have simply disappeared from the archaeological record (Chaplin 1971). The bone breakage damage was caused by carnivore action, trampling and exposure to the elements. The loss of the articular ends was probably due to both carnivore gnawing and frictional action in sediment laden water.

References

Andrews, P (1995) 'Experiments in Taphonomy', *Journal of Archaeological Science* 22, pp. 147-153.

Behrensmeyer, A. (1978) 'Taphonomic and Ecological Information from Bone Weathering', *Paleobiology* 4 (2), pp. 150-162.

Binford, L.R. (1981) *Bones; Ancient Men and Modern Myths.* New York NY: Academic Press.

Chaplin, R.E. (1971) *The Study of Animal Bones from Archaeological Sites,* London: Seminar Press Ltd.

Cohen, A. & D. Searjeantson (1986) *Bird Bones from Archaeological Sites.* London: Archetype Publications Ltd.

Fisher, J.W. (1995) 'Bone Modifications in Zooarchaeology', *Journal of Archaeological Method and Theory* 2 (1).

Grant, A (1975) 'The Animal bones'. In: B.W Cunliffe: with sections by T. Ambrose (*et al*) Ex*cavations at Porchester Castle* Vol. 1, pp. 378-415 (Reports of the Research Committee of the Society of Antiquaries of London: Distributed by Thames & Hudson.

Hillson, S. (1992) *Mammal Bones and Teeth,* Dorchester: Dorset Press.

Lyman, R. (1994) *Vertebrate Taphonomy,* Cambridge: Cambridge University Press.

Marshall, L.G. (1989) 'Bone Modification and "the laws of burial"', in R. Bonnichsen & M.H. Sorg *Bone Modification* pp 7-24, Orono: University Maine Center for the Study of the First Americans.

Schmid, E. (1972) *Atlas of Animal Bones,* Amsterdam - London - New York: Elsevier Publishing Co.

Snails

AS noted above, very little organic material was found although snail shells had survived in huge numbers in the lime marl in certain restricted areas. These were very hard to remove from the lime and Peter Bere spent a considerable amount of time recovering more than a thousand of them. It was an extremely difficult job but he followed up with the equally daunting task of photographing them all under a microscope.

The shells are being studied by Dr Ben Rowsen, Curator of the Department of Biodiversity & Systematic Biology, Amgueddfa Cymru - National Museum Wales (Terrestrial Mollusca). Dr Rowson believes that there are probably around forty different species and that they are mostly terrestrial ones.

The snails were preserved – especially thousands of small or minute ones – concentrated in areas of the marl apparently close to the lake/lagoon edge which seems to suggest that they were sinking to the bottom of still water over a long period. Alternatively they may of course have been gathered together during a period of rising water levels.

Peter Bere, who can put his hand to anything scientific, developed his own sophisticated techniques for removing them from the marl and finally recovered over a thousand specimens. He followed this with an equal number of remarkable photographs taken under the microscope.

A small selection of Peter Bere's photographs of Parc Glyndŵr snails is reproduced on Page 109; all archive pictures have scales.

+   +   +

An unexplained, round-bottomed feature, in the bed of the post-glacial lake had accumulated tens of thousands, possibly millions, of snails. The feature was revealed during peat stripping in Plot 42 which was an area that was near to the edge of the lagoon – as occasionally marked by drifts of snails here and elsewhere on the site.

The suggested sequence is that the depression or cut (off white on the bottom of the photo) existed before the original lake had drained and that the snails began drifting in during the early days of the lagoon which followed. The remains were preserved in a thick layer of lime (not as white as the normal pondweed marl on the site but with the same strong reaction to HCl); there were lots of snails in the primary fill but they built up in incredible numbers just before the formation of the peat [August 2013].

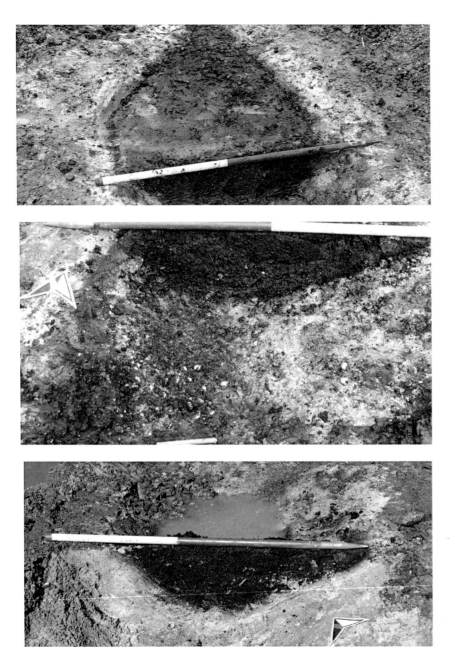

Plot 43. An unexplained feature in the bed of the post-glacial lake: Top–partly excavated with peat fill intact; Middle–Peat removed, showing upper fill (with massed snails); Bottom–lower lime fill (with moderate accumulation of snails) removed to expose the gravel bed of the lake.

APPENDIX A

The Port of Monmouth

By Gordon McDonald

THE last two thousand years has seen the coastal profile of the British Isles vary to a very considerable extent, particularly with regard to river estuaries and tidal inlets. This is not least because during this time there have been three major cycles of tidal progression (including the current one) and two cycles of tidal regression. As if this is not enough post-glacial rebound has complicated the matter, further changing land levels themselves surreptitiously over time, crucially for us in certain tidally sensitive areas. These phenomena combined have distorted what has hitherto been our perception of what was thought to be a more or less stable geography.

Following 43AD, critical to the Roman invasion of Britain, we see not only the establishment of a reliable network of military roads but also the creation of a large number of coastal ports readily accessible from the sea, both for logistic supply and security. The Roman incursion into South Wales resulted in the creation of a string of supply ports from Caerwent to Caerleon, Cardiff and across to Neath and Carmarthen. All these ports had roads heading inland except, it appears, Caerwent whose only main road headed west to the east bank of the Usk at Caerleon. In the gap between Caerleon and Gloucester only Monmouth on the west bank of the River Wye, 13 miles inland from the Severn estuary, has a major route heading north. Significantly, although there is evidence of a Roman road leading to Monmouth from Usk in the early years of the occupation this route would have had serious issues; suggesting construction here may have been well into the 2nd century AD and initially was not the town's main contact with the outside world.

Monmouth's present day site is no stranger to occupying a waterfront environment. The last Great Northern Hemisphere ice sheet created a sculptured and undulating landscape across the whole of the Wye Valley leaving behind low hills of glacial moraines behind which ponded at least one of a series of post-glacial lakes. The first of these was Letton Lake, between Hay on Wye and Hereford, now a broad expanse of flood plain which was at one time a lake of considerable size. The next lake was at Hampton Bishop, four miles to the south-east of Hereford with a third lake below Ross-on-Wye and a fourth lake at Monmouth.

Today, between the Severn estuary and Monmouth the River Wye is tidal for a little under two thirds of its length. Six thousand years ago for a brief period the Monmouth basin, including the Wye's tributary the

Monnow, ceased being what appears to have been a post glacial lake and was inundated from the sea. Recently uncovered evidence now indicates that two thousand years ago the Wye and the Monnow again became tidal for an extended period, a situation which appears to have continued well into the early Roman occupation. A combination of sea level tidal progression and rewinding progressive geological land uplift, it is possible to demonstrate that circa 80AD deep draught Roman merchant ships could not only access in large numbers Caerwent's tidal inlet but also up the River Wye to Monmouth itself.

With average twice monthly spring tides peaking at what is today the 45ft or 13.7 metre contour this would permit the largest shipping of the time having sufficient depth of water underneath their keels at both Caerwent and Monmouth. It would take approximately two days to reach Monmouth from the sea on the twice monthly spring tide cycle, beaching close to the present day Wye Bridge, off loading and reloading over the two week neap tide cycle and then floating off downriver on the next spring tide ebb. Occasional extreme astronomical high spring tides may well have exceeded this and reached the present day 50ft or 15 metre contour, but that would have been the exception, it would have temporarily covered the road to Caerleon just outside Caerwent. However, in Monmouth's case any floodwater in the Wye or Monnow coinciding with a spring tide would have driven river levels significantly higher again. With tides at this level, because any road to Monmouth from Usk has to cross the River Monnow, it would have been initially unusable without a causeway and bridge, as the Romans were forced to construct at Gloucester.

From the middle of the second century AD onwards evidence indicates sea level was already in a long cycle of tidal regression (see CIA Newsletter 59, Falkirk and the Antonine Wall), this would have made shipping access to Monmouth from the sea progressively difficult as the spring tides became shallower. By the 7th century AD it is calculated the River Wye would have been tidal for less than half its distance between Monmouth and the sea. However, nothing stays the same indefinitely and by the 11th century for a period of probably 50 years around 1100AD and possibly as long as 100 years it would have been possible for substantial vessels to once more make their way up the Wye to Monmouth. Once again history as so often happens repeats itself and this time a new invader, the Normans, would have been able to take advantage of the port facility, in their turn undertaking an invasion of Wales. Nevertheless, tidal levels never repeated their peak of 1,000 years earlier and a clue to this is the site chosen for the Norman supply base and stronghold at Caldicot, disregarding the substantial Roman fortifications still remaining at Caerwent, a short distance inland. Crucially, shipping could access

Caldicot when the Norman site was being developed but not Caerwent farther up the shallower tidal inlet.

Without the archaeology our ability to understand how specific locations evolved in their environment would be impossible. At Monmouth not only does the archaeology speak volumes but critically dateable archaeology has been found sealed within the natural geology. Wave formed and tidal strand line beach deposits at quite astonishing levels around the town clearly demonstrate that at various times in the past and in some cases the quite recent past the level of the rivers surrounding the town have flowed much higher in the landscape in a series of successive cycles, a natural process which continues to this day.

It will only take a modest rise in sea level in our current cycle of global warming for Monmouth to become tidal once again. Perhaps a 'Monmouth Marina' will be a serious reality in the coming decades and boat building and chandlery return to the town after an absence of several centuries.

Gordon McDonald, Surveyor, 13th July 2011
Hill Cottage
Dean Road
Newnham on Severn, Gloucestershire

As we were going to Press I e-mailed Gordon: 'Let's see what other interpretations come in' and he e-mailed back:
Don't worry there is no other interpretation.
1. Lakeside location in the Neolithic and Bronze Age.
2. Lake level confirmed by unrelated sites (shoreline like the "parallel roads of Glen Roy").
3. Parallel features orientated at right angles to and running into the lake.
4. Dateable artefacts consistent with boatbuilding coexisting with the identified lake level.
5. Site located adjacent to reliable source of timber suitable for boatbuilding.
6. Monmouth Lake and River Wye a major Ancient navigation with access to the sea.
7. The Lower Wye has been tidal to/below Monmouth since the end of the Middle Stone Age.
8. Extensive recorded evidence for the style of craft the site features allude to.
9. The site was preserved because the lake retreated and it became buried under farmland.
10. Had it not been for Charles Church Parc Glendwr Development it would still be undisturbed.
11. Neolithic & Bronze Age settlements in the Wye Valley suggesting a significant population.
12. Remains of Bronze Age sewn plank boat at Caldicot close the Wye mouth.
1 to 4 is backed up by hard archaeology. 5 to 9 and 12 are corroborative, 10 and 11 subjective.
Regards, Gordon

APPENDIX B - RADIOCARBON DATES

Burnt Mound 1 SO 49289 13131
2292-2121 cal BC, 3765±35 BP   *SUERC-41283 (GU27744)*
August 2012

Burnt Mound 2 SO 49286 13117
2271-2259 cal BC, 3720±35 BP   *SUERC-41283 (GU27745)*
August 2012

Slot across Burnt Mound 3
2201-2011 cal BC, 3700±35 BP   *SUERC-41286 (GU27744)*
July 2012

Burnt Mound 3 with slots SO 49281 13120
2131-2086 cal BC, 3630±35 BP   *SUERC-40354 (GU27742)*
August 2012

Burnt Mound 4
1410-1209 cal BC, 3040±35 BP   *SUERC-4125 (GU27746)*
August 2012

Animal bone on the bed of lake
766-484 cal BC, 2475±35 BP   *SUERC-41290 (GU27748)*
August 2012

Wood on bed of the lake
375-193 cal BC, 2200±29   *SUERC-41738 (GU31245)*
August 2013

Stone Age hearth attenuation pond ST 49286 13117
3637-3500 cal BC, 4745±35 BP   *SUERC-41282 (GU27743)*
August 2012

Silted/sand filled channel
1661-1706 cal BC, 166±30 BP   *SUERC-43780 (GU29088)*
January 2013

Peat drainage channel
176-212 cal BC, 1755±30 BP   *SUERC-39021 (GU26612)*
April 2013

MA17.11 (2)
752-686 cal BC, 2440±30 BP   *SUERC-40260 (GU27214)*
June 2011

Charcoal wood plank? near BM 3
1248-1245 cal BC, 2899±31   *SUERC-40260 (GU30722)*
June 2013

24 St James' St. Below alluvial, A
50BC-80AD, cal 1990±30   *SUERC-32277 (GU22831)*
December 2010

24 St James' St. Below alluvial B
170BC-20AD, cal 2050±30   *SUERC-32278 (GU22832)*
December 2010

APPENDIX C

References

Relevant Works by Gordon McDonald
1...Tidal Aggression 'The Seafarer' 2001
2…The Future for Archaeology, Uncovering the Ancient World 'Independent Archaeology' March 2002
3...In Search of the Flood - The Evidence 'Independent Archaeology' June 2007
4...Falkirk and the Antonine Wall 'Independent Archaeology' August 2007
5...Falkirk Harbour post 143AD 'Independent Archaeology' Spring 2008
6...Severn Estuary River Bank Research 'Independent Archaeology' May 2009
7...Coastal Archaeology ar Risk 'Independent Archaeology' February 2010
8...Lost lakes of the River Wye 'Independent Archaeology' June 2011
9...Port of Monmouth 'Independent Archaeology' April 2012

Prehistoric Archaeology & Prehistoric Boats
Alberti, M. E. & Sabatini. S. 2013. *Exchange Networks and Local Transformations*. Oxbow Books.
Bruck, J. 2011. *Bronze Age Landscapes: Tradition and Transformation*. Oxbow Books.
Clark, P. 2004. *The Dover Bronze Age Boat*. Swindon: English Heritage.
Delage, C. *The Last Hunter-gatherers in the Near East*, British Archaeological Reports.
Eogan, G. 1983. *The Hoards of the Irish Later Bronze Age*. Dublin.
Ferriby Heritage Trust. *Information on the Bronze Age boats found at North Ferriby, East Yorkshire, England, UK.*
Gardiner, R.. 2004. *The Earliest ship: The Evolution of Boats into Ships (Anatomy of the Ship)*. Oxford University Press.
Hall, D. 1994. *Fenland survey: an essay in landscape and persistence/David Hall and John Coles*. London; English Heritage.
Mackereth, F. J. H. *Some chemical observations on post-glacial lake sediments*. The Royal Society. London.
McGrail, S. 2006. *Ancient Boats and Ships*. Shire Publications Ltd.
McGrail, S. 1998. *Ancient Boats in North-West Europe. The Archaeology of Water Transport to AD1500*. Longman.
McGrail, S. 2004. *Boats of the World from the Stone Age to Medieval Times*. Oxford University Press.
McGrail, S. 1978. *Logboats of England and Wales*. British Archaeological Reports Ltd.
Menotti, F. & O'Sullivan, A. 2012. *The Oxford Handbook of Wetland Archaeology*. Oxford University Press.
Parker Pearson, M. (2005) *Bronze Age Britain*. London : Batsford.
Rausing, G. 1984. *Prehistoric boats and ships of northwestern Europe*. CWK Gleerup
Van de Noort, R. 2011. *North Sea Archaeologies. A Maritime Biography, 10,000BC - AD1500*. Oxford University Press.

Wachsmann, S. (2008). *Seagoing Ships and Seamanship in the Bronze Age Levant (Ed Rachal Foundation Nautical Archaeology Series),* Texas A&M University Press.
Waddell, J. 1998. *The Prehistoric Archaeology of Ireland.* Galway.

Burnt Mounds
Barfield, L.H. Hodder, M..A. & Barfield, L.H. 1990 *Hot Stones: Hot Food or Baths?* Papers from the Second International Burnt Mound Conference, Sandwell, Oct 1990
Ehrenberg, M.R. Hodder, M. A. & Barfield, L.H. 1990. *Some Aspects of the Distribution of Burnt Mounds' Burnt Mounds & Hot Stone Technology.*
Jeffrey, P. Barfield, L.H & Hodder, M.A. 1990 *Burnt Mounds, Fulling and Early Textiles*

Rock Art
Beckensall, Stan (1999). *British Prehistoric Rock Art.* Stroud: Tempus.
Bradley, Richard; Chippindale, Christopher; Helskog, Knut (2001). 'Post-Paleolithic Europe'. In David S. Whitley. *Handbook of Rock Art Research.* Lanham: AltaMira Press.
Kaul, F. (1998). *Ships on Bronzes. A Study in Bronze Age Religion and Iconography.* Copenhagen National Museum.
Kristiansen. K. (1998). *Europe before History.* Cambridge, Cambridge University Press.
Kristiansen. K., and Larsson, T (2005). *The Rise of Bronze Age Society. Travel, Transmissions and Transformations.* Cambridge, Cambridge University Press.
Smith, Brian A.; Walker, Alan A. (2011). *Rock Art and Ritual: Mindscapes of Prehistory.* Stroud: Amberley.

General & Local References
Cornwall, I. W. 1966. *Soils for the Archaeologist.* Phoenix House Ltd.
Darwin, C. 1881. *The Formation of Vegetable Mould, through the Action of Worms, with Observations on Their Habits.* Murray.
George, G. T. 2008. *The Geology of South Wales. A Field Guide.* G. T. George.
Godwin, H. *The Archives of Peat Bogs.* Cambridge University Press.
Kissack, K.E. 1974. *Medieval Monmouth.* Monmouth Hist. & Educational Trust.
Kissack, K.E. 1975. *Monmouth, The Making of a County Town.* Phillimore.
Lamb, Hubert H. 1968. *The Changing Climate,* London: Methuen.
Lamb, Hubert H. 1977. *Climatic History and the Future*, Princeton: Princeton University Press, Vol. 2.
Lamb, Hubert H. 1988. *Weather, Climate & Human Affairs: A Book of Essays and Other Papers*, London and New York: Routledge.
Owen, T. R. 2006. *Geology Explained in South Wales.* Fineleaf Editions.
Seale, E. J. 1970. *The Rivers of Monmouthshire. A Geomorphological Study.* Christopher Davies Publishers, Wales.
British Geological Survey. 1970. *South Wales (British Regional Geology)* Stationery Office Books.

INDEX